Sports Illustrated

BACKPACKING

A Complete Guide

Sports Illustrated Winner's Circle Books

BOOKS ON TEAM SPORTS

Baseball
Basketball
Football: Winning Defense
Football: Winning Offense
Hockey
Lacrosse
Pitching
Soccer

BOOKS ON INDIVIDUAL SPORTS

Bowling
Competitive Swimming
Cross-Country Skiing
Figure Skating
Golf
Racquetball
Running for Women
Skiing
Small-Boat Sailing
Tennis
Track: Championship Running
Track: Field Events

SPECIAL BOOKS

Backpacking
Canoeing
Fly Fishing
Scuba Diving
Strength Training

Sports Illustrated

BACKPACKING

A Complete Guide

by Jack McDowell

Sports Illustrated

Winner's Circle Books

New York

Library of Congress Cataloging-in-Publication Data
McDowell, Jack.
  Sports illustrated backpacking: a complete guide / by Jack McDowell.
    p.   cm. — (Sports illustrated winner's circle books)
  Bibliography: p.
  ISBN 0-452-26270-4
  1. Backpacking. 2. Backpacking—Equipment and supplies.
I. Title. II. Series.
GV199.6.M42   1989
796.5'1—dc19   89 90 91 92 AG/HL 10 9 8 7 6 5 4 3 2   89-6061

Contents

Preface

Not so many years ago, just about the only individuals who willingly left cars, beds, and home-cooked meals to "rough it" in the outdoors for days at a time were hunters or scouts. Anyone else who slept on the ground was considered a nut.

Sometime during the mid-1970s, more people became aware of the natural landscape. They began probing deeper into local forests, farther into national forests and parks. Not to hunt, but to enjoy nature. They began to understand how peaceful and how precious the wilderness is.

Today, places close to home are just a beginning. Outdoors people hike from border to border of their own country. Then they take on the globe. They travel to Asia, or South America, or Africa to trek and ramble in mountains, on deserts, along isolated beaches. They meet other hikers.

In so doing, backpackers gain an appreciation for the world around them—the natural world as well as that of their fellow human beings. That is good.

Aside from the uncountable and unnamed trekkers I've come in contact with over the years, I've enjoyed exceptional fellowship with Julie and Tom Harris, Darvel and Daryl Lloyd, Al Senzatimore, Peter Speer, Jon Thomas, and John Watjen. Thanks to them for good times.

For memorable cooperation, thanks to The North Face, Sierra Designs, and The Ski Hut, all in California, and to The Pack Rat, in Arkansas.

Most important of all, thanks to Carole and to Holly for being who they are.

Jack McDowell

Tripping and Trekking

One autumn-cool evening not long ago, while sitting atop a mountain watching alpine glow bathe a neighboring peak in a hue suggestive of rosé wine, I mentioned to my hiking companion that I was writing a book on backpacking.

"What's to write?" he said, zipping up his jacket against the night chill. "Just get out and get on with it."

"But getting on with it is easier if one knows what to expect before beginning," I countered.

"Maybe," said my friend, who is known as a person of few words. "But there's nothing complicated about backpacking."

He's right, of course. There's nothing complicated about backpacking. If I pigeonhole a simple subject into some categories, some basic activities, it's to pass along a lot of information in an uncomplicated way. Wherever you expect to backpack, for whatever length of time, your trip will involve most if not all of the following activities: planning and preparing, garbing and clothing, walking and carrying, navigating and weathering, settling and sheltering, cooking and dining, bedding and slumbering, thriving and surviving.

There are some people who are in a constant state of readiness, who can, without planning, pick

Toting only lightweight backpacks, hiking companions wend their way homeward after a day's outing.

up and head out at a moment's notice. But most of us need *some* preparation so we can at least decide where we want to go and throw together a peanut butter sandwich. Even going at your very lightest—which means taking only the absolute essentials—you'll want some kind of clothing, plus a little extra.

Walking is the accepted mode of travel (the most avid backpacker will curl a lip at the offer of a ride, even though dog-tired). And to keep the hands free for plucking berries, or just swinging at arms' ends, you'll want a pack of some sort. And you'll want some navigational aids so you can tell where you are.

Then, if you expect to spend a night out, you'll take along some sort of shelter. On brilliant nights you may not need anything over you, but if rain pours down you'll want something between it and you.

Some mystics claim they derive nourishment from air and water. If you're one, then food is of no concern to you. On the other hand, most of us mortals burn a lot of energy on the trail, and the best way of renewing that energy is to eat. Eating means food. Not necessarily cooked food, but food. Without it you won't go far.

Energy renewal has to do with sleeping, too. When I was a lad, one of my heroes was Robin Hood. I thought it was really great how after a day of taking from the rich and giving to the poor, Robin and his merry men would wrap up in blankets and throw themselves down on the ground for a good night's sleep. I tried it—in the Midwest, in January. I lasted through the night, but I didn't get any sleep, good or otherwise, and I decided Robin Hoods are a vanishing breed. The line between comfortable sleep and borderline survival is sometimes established by a ground pad and a sleeping bag. You can backpack without either, but you'll enjoy the outdoors more if you have both.

On the subject of thriving and surviving, out in the wild there are quite a few ways the body can be damaged or done in. Though only a chronic worrywart dwells on them, anyone with an ounce of common sense should be prepared to cope with most of them. For the backpacker, being survival conscious can make the difference between life and you-know-what.

Just what *is* backpacking? Everyone has his or her own idea, but for most people, backpacking is carrying on your back everything necessary for self-sufficiency and then using your feet to get it and yourself from one place to another.

WHY PEOPLE BACKPACK

Once over a period of months I made an informal survey among friends and fellow hikers, asking them why they backpacked. Disregarding the few fishy stares the question deserved, the more serious answers proved revealing.

For one thing, people backpack to get away from other people. "It's not that I'm antisocial," said a young woman, "but there are times when it's good to escape voices and personalities for a little while."

Escape from noise is another reason—the noise of cars, and trains, and typewriters, and television. Oh, the backcountry has plenty of sounds, and some of them are weird, especially those heard in the middle of a pitch-black night when your flashlight is just out of reach. But the sounds of nature are somehow more soul soothing than man-made noises.

These "escape" reasons speak of things people try to get away from. What about things people get away *to?*

"I backpack to feel the out-of-doors," said someone else. "Not just to observe or be entertained like a casual tourist, but to *experience* what's happening around me."

Backpacking is a whole series of experiences. It's watching the sun set on the desert; it's drinking from a clean mountain stream; it's stretching out a bone-weary body on a bed of pine needles; it's listening to the sound of rain drumming on a tent. Backpacking is a total commitment. When you're in the wild you're there body and soul, and you're not concerned with the demands of your everyday life.

Other reasons for backpacking? People backpack for exercise, for the challenge of reducing their existence—if only for a little while—to the bare essentials, for a change of pace, to gain a feeling of self-sufficiency, to find themselves, or simply to get from one place to another in the wilderness. Most

Far from the city's bustle, hikers take time to explore a sparkling stream. Having a flexible outdooring schedule that allows for such leisurely diversions enhances the wilderness experience.

of all, people backpack for the sheer fun of it, for the tremendous pleasure it gives them.

Who can backpack? Anyone of any size, age, or profession, as long as they're in reasonable health. In the wild I've met (and sometimes been overtaken by) zealous moppets whose heads hardly reached my hip pocket, as well as sprightly octogenarians, both carrying full packs.

WHAT YOU NEED TO BACKPACK

The basics needed for backpacking are pretty simple. It goes without saying that you should have a desire to spend some time outside. You can't backpack indoors. You have to *want* to be outside. If the thought of sunshine on your face, wind in your hair, and earth under your feet spooks you, backpacking is not for you. And you have to enjoy walking. Remember, our earlier definition of backpacking said something about using your feet.

Some simple equipment is necessary—such as a pair of comfortable, sturdy shoes. Also a few articles of clothing, some food, and something to carry it in. The more involved a trip becomes, the more equipment will be required. But usually far less gear is needed than most people imagine.

Some fundamental knowledge and a few skills won't hinder your backpacking pleasure and will in all likelihood enhance it. For example, if you can recognize the feel of a developing blister, you can avoid getting that blister. And recognizing weather signs can be helpful. Knowing what to do in bad weather can mean the difference between staying dry or being soaked. My first half-dozen backpacking trips were made in superb weather. I'd come to expect it. Then came a trip when rain didn't just fall; it cascaded from the sky. I felt put upon by the elements. Fortunately I had gained a few skills by then and, though I couldn't avoid the rain, I was able to stay sheltered. In backpacking, at least, a little knowledge is not a dangerous thing. And the more knowledge you have, the better off you'll be.

Perhaps as basic as anything else is a healthy respect for nature. That doesn't mean *fear*. If you're really afraid of nature as a whole, you may have problems in the wilderness and might do better at more structured sports. To respect nature is to be concerned about it, to have regard for it, and to accept its ways. The earth and its wild things have been around a lot longer than humankind, and they deserve our consideration.

HOW TO START BACKPACKING

"How do I begin backpacking?" I've been asked. Put some extra clothing and food in a pack and start walking. It's as simple as that. But if you want to know how to cook dinner with an ounce of fuel, or how to sleep comfortably on roots and rocks, or how to coolly toss around impressive words like "trailhead," "benchmark," and "topography," there are other ways to begin backpacking.

You can read books and magazines. There are plenty available. Most backpacking primers cover at least the basics, and from there you can put into practice what you've read. As the slogan of an old mail-order trade school read, "Learn by doing!" Read, but also *do*. Get yourself out on a trail and put the words into practice.

You can take a class. Many high schools, junior colleges, community colleges, and adult education centers offer courses ranging from basic and advanced backpacking to wilderness survival. Such classes usually consist of several hours of lecture culminating in a trip or two. They're informative, and they're fun. If the instructors are at all worth their salt—or their fee—you'll learn a lot about carrying everything on your back while propelling yourself with your feet.

If you enjoy group activities, you might join a regional or national outdooring organization, such as the Appalachian Trail Conference, the Sierra Club, or the Wilderness Society. If you aren't a groupie, hook up with someone who is experienced and has the patience to point things out to a novice. Either is a good way to gain backpacking knowledge and pick up the necessary skills. You can often meet other outdoors people by making yourself known at local outdooring stores.

HIKING CLOSE TO HOME

To find out if you care at all for the idea of walking with a pack on your back, take a day hike. Find a county or state park close to home, a place you can reach in no more than an hour's drive, a place with a trail system for hikers rather than for horses or vehicles. Outfit yourself with a pair of comfortable shoes: hiking shoes if you have them; if not, sneakers will work fine, as long as the trail isn't too rough. Wear loose clothes appropriate for the day's temperature. Into a small pack put a sweater (if the weather is likely to turn cool), a windbreaker, some moleskin (see page 75), scissors, a lunch, and a plastic bottle of water. Don't carry anything in your hands. It throws you off balance and is a nuisance to keep track of.

A short hike on level ground is a good way to enjoy a first taste of backpacking, especially if you're not used to walking. Take plenty of time to savor new sights, new sounds, and then—your appetite whetted—return another day.

After a good breakfast, head out on the trail, hiking at a pace comfortable to you and any companions. Don't charge along at a huff-and-puff rate, but don't loaf either. Sometimes dawdling is nice, perhaps to watch a squirrel or to photograph a sunlit leaf. If you tire, take a ten-minute rest. Any longer, except for lunch break, and you won't feel like walking anymore. When you get hungry, enjoy the sensation for a while before diving into the goodies. Food tastes great when you're genuinely hungry.

A good day hike might last four to six hours and cover up to ten miles. However, distance isn't important. Enjoying yourself is. If the hike is a first-time experience, make it a pleasant one so you'll keep coming back for more.

Until you've acquired some outdooring experience, it's a good idea to stay on or close to a trail. Going cross-country can be rigorous, and before striking up hill and down dale off the beaten path, you should know how to use a compass and handle a topographic map.

THE OVERNIGHT TRIP

With your appetite for the outdoors whetted by a few day hikes, you'll soon be champing at the bit for an overnight trip. To save lugging along more than one bottle of water, pick a campsite where water is available and plan to reach it a couple of hours before dark to give yourself plenty of time to settle in.

In addition to lunch you'll need a few other meals, but since you'll not be going very far for very long you don't have to go super lightweight unless you want the experience of trying a backpacker's packaged meal. Though they cost more than something you choose from the supermarket shelf, they're tasty and idiot-proof to fix. Just tear open a package of freeze-dried chicken stew or turkey tetrazzini, mix with hot water, and in a couple of minutes dinner is ready. If you're a hearty eater, start off with a cup of instant soup and include some whole grain or pumpernickel bread. For breakfast, try instant oatmeal with powdered milk, raisins, and nuts, plus a cup of tea or instant coffee. Lunches can be sandwiches made at home, or cheese and dry salami with more of that pumpernickel bread.

To heat water for dinner and breakfast, you'll need a backpacker's stove. A lightweight mess kit, a cup, a spoon, and a pocketknife complete your kitchen.

For your first overnighter, aim for summertime's fair weather and forget about tents and tarps. Take a ground cloth (a painter's plastic drop cloth is fine,

An overnight trip calls for sleeping gear, breakfast, lunches, and dinner, plus, perhaps, cooking equipment.

Packing in for a week or two means more weight, including plenty of food, fuel, and toilet items. And there must be ample water along the way.

and it's cheap), a foam sleeping pad or lightweight air mattress, and a lightweight sleeping bag.

As for miscellaneous overnight items, include rain gear (in case you're outfoxed by the weather), a roll-end of toilet paper, a small towel, a toothbrush, some adhesive bandages (Band-Aids), an elastic bandage, a flashlight, extra clothing, and a backpack large enough to contain everything. For your first few trips, try to borrow or rent whatever gear you can. It gives you a chance to get a feel for different types and different makes of equipment before buying.

HEADING FOR THE LONG HAUL

What's the difference between an overnight hike and a trek of a week or two? It's mostly a matter of quantity. The longer you're out, the more food you'll need. So you'll either have to carry more grub or have someone deliver it to prearranged sites. Except for food, stove fuel, toothpaste, and toilet paper,

quantities of most items won't vary greatly from that required for a weekend trip.

For me, the greatest difference between a short trip and a long one is in the *quality* of the outdooring experience. It takes two or three days to unwind and get into a rhythm of hiking, resting, eating, sleeping. Carrying and walking muscles tighten, and civilization's cobwebs blow out of my head. From that point on I'm not just a hiker but a living part of the wild country. Not that I turn up my nose at a weekend walk, or even an afternoon stroll, but if two days are good, more are always better.

HIKING ALONE OR WITH OTHERS

It has probably never been written on a stone tablet, but the exhortation "Thou shalt never hike alone" rings down through the years authoritatively enough

Traveling solo in the wilderness is a calculated risk, but solitude offers special rewards for the self-sufficient hiker.

to have become the Eleventh Commandment. Yet many people not only hike alone but spend weeks traveling solo, miles and days away from human contact, enjoying every minute of it. I'm such a transgressor.

"But don't you get lonesome?" I've been asked.

Sure, once in a while I get lonesome. But the feeling doesn't last long. In the wild there's so much to experience that the mind doesn't have time to dwell on itself. Sometimes sharing an experience can be fine; at other times a mood is created that is so personal that the presence of even the most understanding companion can be distracting.

"But what if something happened?"

By "something" is implied, I suppose, breaking a leg, being attacked by a bear, being struck by lightning, falling into a stream, or a dozen other potential mishaps. Anything *could* happen to anyone, alone or with another person. The point is, going alone into the wild is a calculated risk, and I'm willing to take that risk as a trade-off for the joys of solitude.

A few suggestions for the solo backpacker:

1. Let people know where you're going and when you expect to return.
2. Always be careful.
3. When crossing streams, climbing rocky slopes, or hiking below or above cliffs, be especially careful.
4. Carry plenty of food, clothing, and fuel and adequate shelter.
5. Make sure water is available.
6. Consider taking an emergency signal device, such as lightweight flares.
7. At all times maintain a healthy respect for the wilderness.

For many people, going as part of a group is the most comforting way to experience the wilderness. The company of others can often help allay doubts and fears, bolster confidence. It's a good feeling that in an emergency someone is there to minister or go for help.

Members of a group needn't always be perfectly matched as to ability and experience. Variety is the spice of life, and backpacking with a mixed bag of people can be challenging as well as fun. The novices gain in experience, and the old trail hands gain in patience.

Settling down for the night with others can make for a jolly time. In a group you tend to fix meals together, eat together, and do camp chores together. Being basically social animals, most of us find sharing such mundane tasks satisfying.

The group experience implies cooperation. Whereas a person going solo needs at least one of everything—shelter, stove, mess kit—two or more hikers can cut back on certain gear and divvy up the lugging of it. For example, two people can be quite cozy buddying in a single tent. And in packing the shelter, the tent can go to one person, the poles and stakes to the other. Meal preparation can be shared on an alternate-day basis, but in the touchy area of cooking there should be a gentleman's agreement about not complaining—at least not loudly.

Unless most group members are greenhorns, designating a leader isn't necessary. An experienced easy-to-get-along-with leader is a joy, but an authoritarian martinet is a pain. Unfortunately, you can't always read a person's character in advance. If a trip begins to sour because of a landlocked Captain Bligh or, worse yet, an incompetent, you can either suffer through it or mutiny and elect a new chief.

Each morning the day's plans should be discussed by the entire group and a definite starting time agreed upon. On the move, the strongest member should

Group backpacking usually means sharing camp chores—such as meal preparation and cleanup. It also creates an elemental kind of fellowship.

bring up the rear to keep watch for stragglers and give them a helping hand. Either on or off trail, both the first and the last person should have maps.

Although company can be nice on the trail, the whole group should not cluster together like a flock of sheep, as chatter has a way of dulling the wilderness experience. Rather, members should travel in subgroups of two or three, strung out with plenty of space between individuals. However, everyone should meet at a designated time and place for lunch.

There are some drawbacks to group backpacking. Be prepared to adjust your pace to that of the slowest member (if *you* turn out to be the slowest member, you'll be ever so grateful). Be prepared to chip in with food, water, and such to help the inevitable forgetful member. And be prepared to help shoulder part of another's load.

Even when traveling with close companions in the wilderness, there are places that are best experienced in silence, times when words are unnecessary.

HIKING WITH CHILDREN

Backpacking with youngsters is an entirely different form of the sport, one imposing certain limitations on adults but providing them with an entirely new dimension of outdooring pleasure. The thing to remember is that children are children and not grown-ups, and they cannot be expected to behave like grown-ups. Adults can push themselves to certain limits and will often put up with discomfort without any exterior signs other than a grunt or subdued groan. But most kids are not about to prove anything to anyone, including their parents. If they become uncomfortable, everyone will know about it fast.

Most youngsters are receptive to the fun of being outdoors, and their enjoyment is infectious.

A youngster's attention span is only a fraction of an adult's, and this must be taken into account when backpacking with children. It means you can't walk as long, or sit as long, or sleep as long as you probably would if you were with other adults.

The great outdoors can be overwhelming to a child initially exposed to it, so the first few times out with a youngster, hike in a more or less familiar area not too far from home. Take short day hikes in the beginning, not overnighters. Give the small fry time to adjust to new spaces, new sights, and new sounds, and to the idea of walking to get somewhere (after all, isn't that what cars are for?).

Of course, infants and toddlers aren't yet walkers. But wee ones can be carried Japanese-style in a fabric sling, or papoose-fashion in a metal-frame seat. A well-equipped outdooring store will usually stock small carriers. When toting a child in such rigs, avoid pushing your way through dense brush, and beware of low tree branches. Either can sweep back into the child's face.

Infants will require a good supply of diapers, and if you opt for the disposable variety, do not dispose of them in the backcountry but pack them out with you in a plastic bag.

As for clothing for baby, you won't find outfitters catering to infants, so take along whatever the little one wears at home. Just make sure you bring plenty of it. The same goes for food. Take formula, or baby food, or whatever else the child is accustomed to eating.

At night baby can share space between you and your partner in a double sleeping bag, at the risk of being slightly squashed. Or you can bundle baby up in a sleeping sack fashioned from adult sweaters and a jacket.

From about age three, kids can provide their own locomotion, at least most of the time. But don't expect the younger ones to walk either for very long or in a straight line. After all, the outdoors is a wondrous new place, filled with all kinds of exciting diversions. Keep youngsters under constant surveillance, for, like cats, they can disappear in the blink of an eye. If your small one is especially energetic and has a tendency to dart off the trail, you might consider a leash-and-harness arrangement.

Youngsters six to ten years of age will probably walk *your* legs off. Be prepared to alter your pace to match theirs, but also to slow them down if they are overextending themselves. Children this age can hoist their own pint-sized

When backpacking with children, walk slowly, rest often, and allow plenty of time for them to adjust to new surroundings.

pack, but weighing down a child with too heavy a load can turn a trip into a nightmare for all concerned and can damage soft bones and undeveloped muscles. A pack weight equal to no more than one fourth of the child's weight is enough. *You* carry the rest.

Walking kids can wear whatever they wear when running around at home: sturdy jeans, sneakers, a T-shirt in warm weather, long sleeves, a sweater, a jacket in cool weather. Food is no problem, as long as you bring enough. They'll eat whatever you eat, and most likely more of it. Pre-teenagers can bed down in junior-sized or short-length adult sleeping bags.

GETTING TO KNOW THE MOUNTAINS

Mountains are the result of tremendous deformations of the earth's exterior shell. Some mountains are formed chiefly by folding of the earth's crust, some mainly by faulting (a process of fracturing and displacement), some by violent volcanic eruption. Combinations of these activities are more common than single processes, and in most parts of the world the building of mountains goes on continuously, too slowly to be observed by the backpacker but quite measurable by geologists.

The Appalachians are mostly folds that have been eroded to long parallel ridges; the Colorado and Wyoming Rockies are folded structures; the Sierra Nevada and Wasatch ranges are super fault structures, characterized by crustal blocks that have fractured and slipped past one another; California's Mount Shasta, parts of the Cascade Range, and many of the Alaskan ranges are volcanic mountains, created by eruptive action.

Mountains are the world's high places. They're mostly up-and-down country. You'll swear there's more up than down, but things only seem that way, especially to flatlanders who may be experiencing the mountains close for the first time.

You might as well get used to this fact right from the beginning. Unless you happen to live on top, or are set down on top from the air, the first part of any mountain trek is going to be pretty much uphill. Still, you can console yourself with the sweet thought that what goes up eventually comes down, including your own weary body.

In approaching mountains from the plains or plateaus surrounding them, you'll usually encounter foothills first—low mounds of land, often covered with grasses or forest, that nuzzle against a mountain's base like hungry kittens around their mother. Because these hill reaches are for the most part gentle and rolling, hiking them can be pleasurable.

In mountain country the gentle foothills, dense woodlands, and smooth meadows lead higher into more rugged terrain.

In the lower terrain of a mountain, you'll be hiking through a varied landscape that may range from dry brushland to patches of forest to deep woods. As you move into higher altitudes the atmosphere and forests will thin out, until you reach the upper limits of tree growth. Above timberline, it's mostly rock underfoot and all around. Some backpackers prefer to stay in the lower elevations, in the green coolness of forest shade. Others chug on through all that, unfulfilled until they reach the sparsity of the upper altitudes. I have a friend who virtually runs up a mountainside—full pack and all—not really content until he's left behind the last tree. Only on stark, clean granite does he slow enough to savor the air and gaze around in full appreciation of his surroundings.

This friend is also wise in the ways of finding water up there, which is not always an easy undertaking. There's usually water to be had in the mountains (or else you shouldn't be there), but it doesn't gush forth from every rock. You have to learn its signs.

Mountains with glaciers or snow packs usually have abundant water in the form of ponds, lakes, or streams. But even if a map indicates a stream in a certain site, you may not find it there during certain times of the year. Though you often must depend on a map for locating water, it's always a good idea to inquire locally before setting off. Remember, water is all-important. Without it you can't get very far or last for very long.

In truly high country, snow pack may remain year round, which usually means there is plenty of water for backpacking. But it also may mean cold nights and more challenging hiking.

Mountain country doesn't have many creatures that are overly bothersome to humans. Bugs and mosquitoes? Yes, in lower-altitude woodsy areas they can be annoying during warm weather. But bugs are a minor nuisance that can be endured, or at least minimized with a good insect repellent. Some foothills and low mountains are host to snakes, and mere thought of the slithery things is enough to keep many people out of the woods. However, except for a very few dangerous varieties, most snakes are harmless and are more anxious to avoid you than you are them. (More on this later.)

Many mountainous regions, as well as some of the northern forests, are the home of bears, and bears—whether they are grizzlies, browns, or blacks—are not to be trifled with. Reading up on bears will help you understand their behavior, but there is no guarantee you'll never encounter one. In starting off at a trailhead, question park rangers or other hikers for "bear news." Ask if any bears have been spotted, if any people have been bothered, if any areas are best avoided. While hiking, be alert for areas with bear tracks or droppings, and give such areas a wide berth.

Like most wild creatures, bears would just as soon avoid humans, so make some noise to let them know of your presence. Constant singing or whistling isn't necessary, and a portable radio will simply not do in the backcountry. Instead, tie a small bell to your pack to announce your presence. The sound may drive you batty, but it'll tell any bears around that *you* are around too.

Steep mountain slopes may be covered with loose rock or snow that can suddenly let go and move downward in a scouring, rushing avalanche. Learning to recognize potential avalanche areas (smooth, convex, leeward slopes of 30 to 45 degrees), and steering clear of them, is the best way to avoid that danger.

The complex subject of avalanches is under continual study worldwide. If you expect to pass through avalanche regions, better check the writings on the topic. Some titles are listed at the back of this book.

GETTING TO KNOW THE DESERT

Painted perhaps by too many late late movies, the classical image of a desert is a sandy waste of shifting dunes rolling on to a limitless horizon, a lifeless place scorched bare by a relentless sun. This image may hold for a few regions, but obviously they all have boundaries, many are not sandy, many aren't even hot, and none of them are lifeless. Parts of the Arctic are classified as desert, for the word desert merely denotes a terrain that receives less than ten inches of rainfall annually.

Despite its dryness, a desert's landscape is shaped mainly by streams. In

In the spring the desert is at its best, at least for backpacking. Temperatures are mild during the day and cool at night, water is generally available, and wildflowers are a visual feast. But beware the cactus. Carelessly brushing against one can be a painful encounter.

a desert, rains are infrequent but heavy, and they produce torrents that carve the hard-packed ground into gullies and ravines that channel the runoff into larger valleys. In addition, winds sweeping across the flat, arid land erode rocks and shift sand, leaving little foothold for plants.

Because deserts have few springs, and water tables are usually far below the surface, hiking in such areas isn't a casual affair. You must have ample water for the time you expect to be there. For anything more than a day's hike you must be assured of a supplemental water source, such as previously hidden stores (caches) or air drops.

Desert temperatures can soar well above 100 degrees Fahrenheit (38 degrees Celsius) during the day, only to plummet to freezing at night. Rains may be uncommon, but when they do occur—even in nearby mountains—walls of water may rage down gullies, sweeping boulders, cars, tents, and backpackers along like matchsticks. A precaution: If you make camp in the desert, make it on high ground.

Are there unfriendly critters in the desert? Mostly snakes, scorpions, and a few stinging or biting bugs. The best protection against snake bite or scorpion sting is to avoid an encounter altogether. Don't put your hands or feet anywhere without looking first, and always wear hiking boots and long pants. I've known only two hikers who have been bitten by rattlers, and in both cases human carelessness was the cause. Both hikers became a bit ill, but they recovered and now know better. Such emergencies are discussed in chapter 9.

Obviously the desert isn't everyone's cup of tea. Those who are attracted to it love the vast, open skies, the clean air, the primitive desolation, the moods that change with every passing hour. They love the serenity and the silence, for they realize that despite its seeming hostility, the desert is a fragile place needing protection from humans instead of the other way around. It *is* a harsh environment to some, but it is also a delicate one. Treat it gently.

GETTING TO KNOW YOURSELF

A hot slog up a steep trail can encourage some fancy flights of the imagination, anything to avoid dwelling on the matters at hand, whether they be aching shoulders, a blistered heel, or a parched throat.

Despite its physical demands, backpacking turns out to be a contemplative pastime. On the trail I'm forever ruminating on moment-to-moment impressions—the feeling of earth underfoot, the forest sounds, the outdoor smells. Some people cogitate on the happenings of the day, some on the expectations

Happy is the outdoors person who is comfortable being alone and delights in spending time close to nature.

of the morrow. Others think about the mess they left the house in, or the work they have to return to on Monday. The point is, whatever you think about, you end up spending a lot of time inside your own head.

Some people aren't used to being alone with their own thoughts, and this intimidates them. What's worse is that it can make them leery of backpacking, and they spend their time worrying instead of having a good time.

If you're the worrying kind, maybe you're better off doing something with a little more structure and with enough diversions to take your mind off your problems. If you're not the worrying kind, or if you think you can control your thoughts enough so that you'll only dwell on positive things, more power to you. Backpacking might just be *the* pastime for you.

TREATING THE LAND KINDLY

No two ways about it, the wild lands of the world are in danger—not from natural causes alone but from humans, who have a tendency to change, re-arrange, or develop for the likes of highways, stores, and paved parking lots. No need to go into what is or isn't "progress," other than to say that often under its guise a lot of the natural world is damaged, even destroyed.

But if you can't halt progress (just as you can't fight City Hall), you as a backpacker can help to reduce humanity's impact on the wilderness. For example, if you set up a campsite in the vicinity of a pleasant stream, enjoy that stream for what it is and don't go damming it with rocks to make a swimming hole just as a convenience to your hot body.

Being the thinkingest of all creatures, most of us humans have come a long way from when we squatted half naked on the ground and poked a fire to roast a haunch of buffalo. Now, supposedly, we're civilized. But when we get into the backcountry, away from our television sets and cars and other conveniences, we need to feel once more some of that primitive kinship with nature.

Millions of people camp in the wilderness each year, and most of them try to be careful about the land. But we need to be constantly aware of the fragile relationship between human beings and nature and make efforts to leave as few traces as possible of our having been in the wild.

The technique of traveling light is mostly a matter of learning to feel at home outdoors under almost any conditions without setting up an elaborate camp. The most carefree backpackers are those knowledgeable ones who keep themselves uncluttered and unencumbered. With a minimum of equipment they can go almost anywhere, and the land hardly knows they've been there.

Too much foot traffic over the same route can hasten its erosion by water runoff, transforming a pleasant trail into an unsightly ditch.

Not many of us are John Muirs, willing and able to subsist on crackers and tea, but the idea of "less is better" does seem to be the best guideline for living in the wilderness.

Another way to treat the land kindly is in your choice of campsite. Meadows, lakeshores, and streamsides are lovely places, but their fragile soil cannot hold up under the use of campers. Once ruined, it may never restore itself.

A roaring bonfire was once considered an essential part of being outdoors. How chummy it was to sit around the evening campfire, singing songs and toasting marshmallows. But today the wilderness can't support many campfires. Living trees are a precious resource, and dead wood is a part of the natural landscape. Cooking can be done more quickly and efficiently over a backpacking stove than over an open fire anyway, so why not use a stove and preserve the landscape? Save the marshmallows for home or for established campsites.

Of course, if a fire is needed to dry clothing or prevent chilling, then you should build one. (We'll get into this more in chapter 7.) But don't build it against cliffs or large boulders where it can permanently discolor the rocks and announce to everyone who follows that you've already been there. And when you break camp after having had a fire, eradicate all traces by pulverizing the dead ashes, mixing them with loose soil, and scattering them.

Pure water is one of the rare joys of the outdoors, so protect it from soap and other sources of pollution and never wash cooking or eating utensils

Unpolluted water is rare in the wilderness. Avoid washing yourself or your utensils directly in lakes or streams, and keep all waste at least 50 yards away from any water.

Litter ruins the wilderness experience for everyone. Heed the hiker's cardinal rule: **Carry out what you carry in.** At the trailheads in many parks are waste containers. Dispose of trash there rather than along the trail.

directly in a lake or stream. Few wilderness experiences are as sadly memorable as filling a water bottle in a sparkling brook, only to see a cheese-covered noodle drift into the container.

Locate latrines at least 50 yards from water, or from a camping area, burying all solid wastes six inches or so below the surface, where they'll quickly decompose.

Organic garbage can be scattered on the ground, away from water and camp and out of sight. Wildlife will dispose of it, or it will decay and return to the soil. Orange peels are an exception. Animals won't eat them, and they take forever to decompose. Rather than leaving orange peels to be seen by someone else, bury them or pack them out.

High-altitude latrine with a view, not uncommon in the wilderness. While some might dispute its esthetics, it nevertheless reduces pollution in a heavily used area.

Paper and cardboard can be disposed of by burning, and smelly or oily cans and foil can be cleaned in a small fire and then crushed and packed out.

As touchy a subject as religion or politics is that of pet dogs in the backcountry. For every outdoors person who condemns the idea of dogs on the trail there is a pet lover who will raise a hue and cry at the mere suggestion of leaving that pet at home.

Some state and federal parks prohibit dogs; others require them to be leashed. Before setting out on a trek with man's best friend, find out and heed the restrictions.

If you do take your pet into the woods with you—and a dog can be a good companion—make sure you're in control at all times. When other people are on the trail close by, keep the dog at your side; its friendly overtures may not be appreciated by everyone. And at night encourage it to sleep. Your pet's barking may be music to your ears, but it's sure to be a nuisance to others. And if your dog fouls the trail or a camping area, bury the evidence as a courtesy to other hikers.

"Getting away from it all" is, for many people, one of the whys of backpacking, even if getting away means simply sitting in solitude to read a book.

Planning and Preparing

Anything can trigger the primal urge to get outdoors and go—a photograph of a sun-dappled forest, a whiff of crisp air, or the crackle of autumn leaves underfoot. If you're like me, once your button is pushed, you'll grow increasingly restless, moping around and snarling at family and friends until you can start preparing for your trip.

Planning is part of the fun too, especially if you go about it in some organized fashion. A hoary canon still drilled into the heads of cub journalists—in the interests of organization—is that of establishing right off in a story the five *w*s: who, what, where, when, and why. With a couple of variations and an addition or two, this rule can be a fitting beginning for planning your first—or your hundred and first—backpacking trip.

Usually the prime thing to enter your roaming fancy is *where* to go. That quiet stretch of woods in the next county? The bottom end of the Appalachian Trail? The high Rockies? Maybe you have a definite place in mind right off, or maybe you're wide open, just knowing you've got to get out and not caring where you go. But eventually nailing down a "where" is important to the rest of your planning so you don't drift around like a ship with a broken rudder.

When you go depends on how soon you can board out the cat, bolt the door, and take off. It also depends on the kind of weather you want or are willing to put up with. Generally speaking, and averaging the climate over the entire United States, springtime is fresh, cool, and tending to showers and occasional windiness; trees are leafing out, flowers bloom, and life is bursting out all over. Summer can be hot, muggy, and buggy, yet pleasant in most parts except the desert, where the wise hiker would think twice about venturing during July and August. With autumn come cooler days and nights, color changes that delight an artist's eye, and the possibility of early snowfall. Winter is cold-weather time everywhere; then you might experience heavy rains, deep snows, or howling storms, but, depending on where you are, you may also have the clearest skies of the year.

Why you want to stretch your legs over the wild lands has to do mostly with your personal feelings, and unless your trek is to be some kind of expedition, the "why" has probably already asserted itself and doesn't much enter into the mechanics of planning.

The *what* of a trip does. What kind of trip do you have in mind? What is its objective (this of course will be tied up with "why")? Are you going to just ramble in a certain area for a specified time? Are you going to do a loop trip, keeping constantly on the move? Are you going to pack in somewhere, make camp, and spend the allotted days relaxing right there? Are you going to bag a crag or nail a trail? Defining your objective may seem clinical, but it's a great help in estimating amounts of food needed and deciding what equipment will be necessary.

Lastly, *who* else, if anyone, is going? This is another decision affecting provisioning as well as your peace of mind. If the trip is going to be a multi-person affair, you'll need to choose compatible companions. Differences of opinion among members of a group are inevitable and healthy, but if someone is an inveterate crybaby or is constantly in need of a wet nurse, the trip will be hell for everyone. I have shirt-off-my-back buddies I'd lend my dog and car to, but never would we venture into the wilds together, for within five minutes of trailhead we'd be at each other's jugulars. On a backpacking trip people get tired, hungry, hot, and cranky, not infrequently all at the same time. Those are times that try men's and women's souls, so start out with the odds in your favor.

So much for the five *w*s of planning. Add to them a couple of essential *how*s and your scheme of action is well under way. *How long* do you expect to be out, and *how far* do you expect to travel? One factor is time, the other distance, and they are interrelated. The longer you hike, the farther you go (or, the more miles you cover, the more time it takes). The more time and distance, the more provisions needed, and so on.

Abounding with game fish, many wilderness streams lure fisherman hikers willing to backpack many miles to wet a line.

Stalking a subminiature bloom, an outdoorsman of the "wet belly" school of photography gets eye to eye with nature.

"Let's go **here**!" Trip
planning starts at home,
where everyone can voice
an opinion as to destination
and routes.

BEFORE THE TRAILHEAD

Before hoisting your loaded pack and pointing your hiking boots into the woods, there are several things you can do—and should do—right at home to ensure a minimum of hassles later. Right off you can gather information about the area in which you want to trek. Start by reading everything you can lay eyes on: in books, magazines, and other publications. If your area of interest is administered by federal forces, check locally first to find out if there is a nearby headquarters handling information for National Parks, Forests, or Monuments (look in the telephone directory under U.S. Government). Or write one or more of the following agencies:

National Park Service
U.S. Department of the Interior
Washington, D.C. 20240

Forest Service
U.S. Department of Agriculture
Washington, D.C. 20250

Bureau of Sport Fisheries and Wildlife
U.S. Department of the Interior
Washington, D.C. 20240

Bureau of Land Management
U.S. Department of the Interior
Washington, D.C. 20240

Contact state and regional parks, local or national conservation groups, and wilderness travel organizations (such as National Audubon Society, Nature Conservancy, Friends of the Earth, Sierra Club, Wilderness Society, Appalachian Trail Conference, Federation of Western Outdoor Clubs, American Forestry Association). Inquire at commercial outfitters and stores specializing in outdooring gear. Talk with persons who have been in the area recently. Outdoors people may not be the most gregarious types in the world, but generally they are willing to share information and experiences.

Somewhere in the process of doing this homework, begin looking at atlases and trail guides, studying maps that cover the country between you and the trailhead, deciding how you'll get to the trailhead (public transportation, car, or other) and how much time you want to spend at it. If you plan to drive, lay out a route on a road map. Usually it will be the shortest distance between two points, unless you want to sightsee along the way. Decide where you'll leave your car while you're in the wild. Once all that's well in hand you'll be ready for topographic maps.

Studying Topographic Maps

You know what a map is—a flat, symbolic picture of part of the earth's surface as seen by a bird with no depth perception. So how can a flat picture indicate a ridge, which sticks up, or a gully, which dips down? A topographic map does this with contour lines; that is, lines of equal elevation. Many maps (such as road maps and Forest Service maps) don't show contours, but as a hiker you are interested mainly in those that do indicate the landscape's ups and downs. You'll want topographic maps, also called topos or quads.

The scheme of a topo map is simple: Where contour lines (shown in brown) are close together, the terrain is steep; where they're spaced out, the terrain is gentle. Every fifth line is heavier than those in between and is printed with the elevation of that contour.

On most detailed topo maps of mountainous areas, the contour interval —the space between any pair of lines—represents 40 feet. Such maps, called 7½-minute maps, are drawn to a scale of 1:24,000. That means any unit on the map, such as an inch or a foot, represents 24,000 of the same units on the ground. Thus, approximately 2½ inches of map equals one mile of horizontal distance on land. (For some areas, 15-minute maps are available. They show the same detail, but four times as much area and therefore more landmarks.)

In addition to terrain steepness and gentleness, what else can you tell by looking at the contour lines of a topo map? Contour "fingers" pointing at each

TOPOGRAPHIC MAP SYMBOLS

VARIATIONS WILL BE FOUND ON OLDER MAPS

Primary highway, hard surface

Secondary highway, hard surface

Light-duty road, hard or improved surface

Unimproved road

Road under construction, alinement known

Proposed road

Dual highway, dividing strip 25 feet or less

Dual highway, dividing strip exceeding 25 feet

Trail

Railroad: single track and multiple track

Railroads in juxtaposition

Narrow gage: single track and multiple track

Railroad in street and carline

Bridge: road and railroad

Drawbridge: road and railroad

Footbridge

Tunnel: road and railroad

Overpass and underpass

Small masonry or concrete dam

Dam with lock

Dam with road

Canal with lock

Buildings (dwelling, place of employment, etc.)

School, church, and cemetery

Buildings (barn, warehouse, etc.)

Power transmission line with located metal tower

Telephone line, pipeline, etc. (labeled as to type)

Wells other than water (labeled as to type) . . . . oOil. . . . . oGas

Tanks: oil, water, etc. (labeled only if water) . . . . •● Water

Located or landmark object; windmill

Open pit, mine, or quarry; prospect

Shaft and tunnel entrance

Horizontal and vertical control station:

 Tablet, spirit level elevation . . . . BM△5653

 Other recoverable mark, spirit level elevation . . . . △5455

Horizontal control station: tablet, vertical angle elevation VABM △95/9

 Any recoverable mark, vertical angle or checked elevation △3775

Vertical control station: tablet, spirit level elevation . . . . BM✕957

 Other recoverable mark, spirit level elevation . . . . ✕954

Spot elevation . . . . ✕7369   ✕7369

Water elevation 670   670

Boundaries: National

 State

 County, parish, municipio

 Civil township, precinct, town, barrio

 Incorporated city, village, town, hamlet

 Reservation, National or State

 Small park, cemetery, airport, etc.

 Land grant

Township or range line, United States land survey

Township or range line, approximate location

Section line, United States land survey

Section line, approximate location

Township line, not United States land survey

Section line, not United States land survey

Found corner: section and closing

Boundary monument: land grant and other

Fence or field line

Index contour . . . . Intermediate contour

Supplementary contour . . . . Depression contours

Fill . . . . Cut

Levee . . . . Levee with road

Mine dump . . . . Wash

Tailings . . . . Tailings pond

Shifting sand or dunes . . . . Intricate surface

Sand area . . . . Gravel beach

Perennial streams . . . . Intermittent streams

Elevated aqueduct . . . . Aqueduct tunnel

Water well and spring . . . . Glacier

Small rapids . . . . Small falls

Large rapids . . . . Large falls

Intermittent lake . . . . Dry lake bed

Foreshore flat . . . . Rock or coral reef

Sounding, depth curve . . . . 10 . Piling or dolphin

Exposed wreck . . . . Sunken wreck

Rock, bare or awash; dangerous to navigation

Marsh (swamp) . . . . Submerged marsh

Wooded marsh . . . . Mangrove

Woods or brushwood . . . . Orchard

Vineyard . . . . Scrub

Land subject to controlled inundation . . . . Urban area

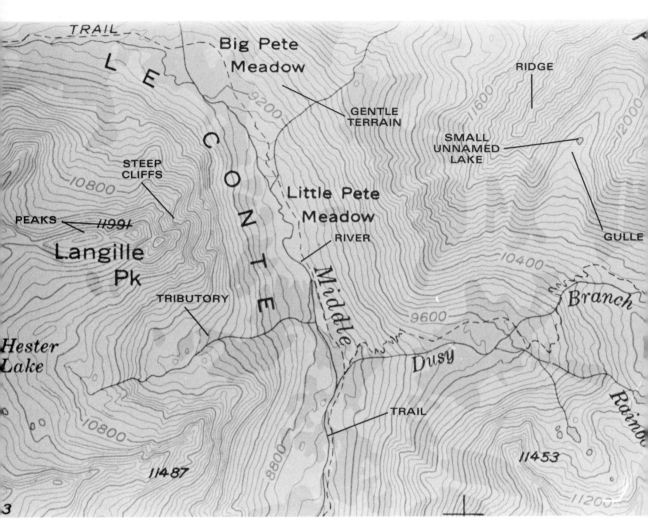

At first glance a topographic map may seem only a mass of squiggly lines, but the meaning of it all becomes clear with the U.S. Geological Survey's list of symbols.

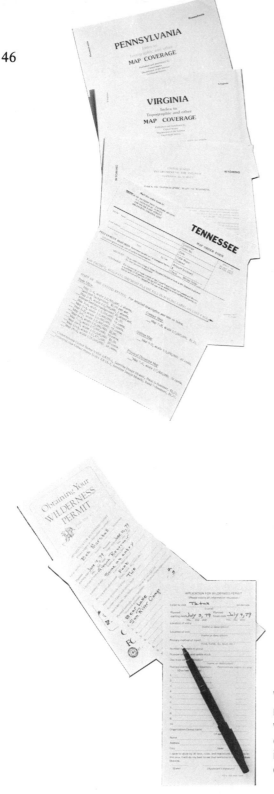

Topographic indexes listing maps that are available for each state can be ordered from the U.S. Geological Survey.

Itinerary for Murphy Mountain Trip

4/3 - 4/4   Drive to Randville. Final organization of gear, compass practice. Stay overnight at State Park.

4/5   After ranger station check-in, to Rubble Meadows via Indian Springs Trail.

4/6   Ascend to timberline around "The Hump." Camp at 6500 feet.

4/7   Spend day on Gravel Glacier. Return to Base Camp.

4/8   High traverse to Lost Lakes. Camp at Lake #3.

4/9   Via Sky Trail, descend to Sunset Camp at Lake Kumquat.

4/10 - 4/11   Fishing and loafing at Lake Kumquat.

4/12   Pack out on Windy Trail. Spend night at Maudie's Motel (Randville). Hot showers!!

4/13 - 4/14   Drive Home.

An itinerary helps solidify your trip planning and lets people know where you are. Carry a copy with you, and leave another with someone at home.

Wilderness permit applications require data on entry and exit as well as your best estimate of camping locations. The information helps prevent overuse of popular backpacking areas.

other indicate a saddle in a ridge, which might be interpreted as a fair campsite. Bunched or pinched-off lines mean a sheer cliff—a good place to hike around unless you're a wall climber. Lines forming a V whose base points toward higher elevations mean a valley or streambed. A U with its base pointing toward lower elevations means a ridge.

Because topo maps also show water features (in blue), man-made features (in black), and woodlands (in green), they are essential for the outdoors person. Topo index maps, published for every state, and a booklet describing symbols are free upon request from U.S. Geological Survey, Washington, D.C. 20242, or Federal Center, Denver, Colorado 80225. The indexes give map prices. Use the indexes to choose detailed maps for the area you're interested in, then order as follows:

Maps of areas east of the Mississippi River, including Minnesota, Puerto Rico, and the Virgin Islands of the United States, should be ordered from Branch of Distribution, U.S. Geological Survey, 1200 South Eads Street, Arlington, Virginia 22202. Maps of areas west of the Mississippi River, including Alaska, Hawaii, Louisiana, American Samoa, and Guam, should be ordered from Branch of Distribution, U.S. Geological Survey, Box 25286 Federal Center, Denver, Colorado 80225.

You can also buy topo maps from some outdooring and mountaineering stores, certain sporting goods shops, and commercial map distributors.

A necessity in the backcountry, topo maps are invaluable in preparing for your trip. With them you can choose routes, plan campsites, determine water availability, and even locate existing trails.

Drawing Up an Itinerary

Itineraries may seem contradictory to the whole idea of roaming free as a deer, but these route plans help to organize your thinking and can be useful to others in the unlikely event that they have to come looking for you. An itinerary doesn't have to be absolutely binding. Depending on local conditions or your state of mind, you can deviate from it without sending carrier pigeons home bearing the tidings.

For weekend trail trips an itinerary need be no more than a route established in your head, with a guess as to starting and stopping hours so you're not stumbling around in the dark while yet miles from camp or trailhead. For longer trips or for off-trail forays, plot a tentative route right on a topo map indicating possible campsites and dates you expect to be there. Then, before telling the folks at home good-bye, leave a written copy of your itinerary with family or friends. It's not that anyone wants to pry into your affairs. It's to let people know where to look for you, should your return be overdue. You'll need to give this information anyway if you apply for a wilderness permit, so keep it at hand.

On the subject of permits: They are almost always needed for backpacking in designated wilderness areas, often required in national parks, and sometimes called for in national forests. You can request a permit by mail from the proper agency, or you can obtain one in person from the field office nearest the area of your interest. Be advised that if you meet with a ranger in the wild and you can't produce a permit, you may be fined.

Itineraries and permits notwithstanding, your plans should allow for options and contingencies. Maybe you become so enamored of that campsite near Lake Kumquat you'll want to stay there for three nights instead of two. Maybe an incessant rain slows your five-mile-a-day pace to three miles. Maybe a slope that looked gentle on the map turns out to be murderous and you decide to walk around a mountain instead of over it. Well, all that is part of outdooring. Just hang loose and be prepared for any such happenings.

Practicing for Backpacking

I can hear it now: "*Practice* backpacking? Stuff and nonsense! All you do is get out and go."

True for most trips, true for old trail hands, for whom the mechanics of backpacking are second nature. But for the myriads of outdooring enthusiasts still a bit green at the game, a little pre-trip training can pay dividends. For example, consider your precious body. If your only exercise is hoisting the evening libation, and you expect to walk away from a nine-to-five desk job and onto the trail, some conditioning may be in order.

You needn't go so far as jogging with a brick-laden pack, as does a dedicated fellow I know. Some mild physical activity for a week or two prior to the trip should fill the bill. Especially important is walking around while wearing your hiking shoes, even if they have been broken in. Feet, legs, and leather will marry harmoniously, minimizing the chance of nagging blisters and sore muscles when you're supposed to be getting next to nature.

Of course, if you're a regular jogger, or if you do a bit of stiff walking during the work week, you're probably in fair condition for backpacking.

Then there's pack loading. A few days before the start of a trip, organize all your gear and stow it in the pack. Now look at the pack for a while and imagine a few not-so-unlikely situations in the wild. A sudden rainstorm? You

Tent-pitching practice at home pays off, especially if your shelter is new. Make sure all poles, stakes, and guy lines are accounted for and all closures are in good working order.

Pack-loading practice helps you realize what you **don't** need. Several sessions may be in order for you to work out the most efficient system of stowage.

really don't want the rain gear at the very bottom. A burning thirst on the trail? Maybe the canteen would be better stowed in an outside pocket instead of buried under your extra shirt.

Get the idea? In the privacy of your own home, practice loading and reloading your gear a few times. Of course, during the first couple of days out you'll be re-jiggering things anyway, but problems anticipated early on will be effort and time saved later.

In the backyard, set up your shelter and break it down once or twice, keeping a sharp eye open for rips, tears, weakened seams, or frazzled guy lines. Imagine yourself pitching the thing in a gale-force wind at night. Are all poles, stakes, and lines accounted for? Are zippers working smoothly? This kind of checkout is essential if you're using a brand-new shelter for the first time. Find out what's needed when you're at home, rather than realizing it in the back-country.

And of course you'll fire up your stove to forestall the chance of its balking the first time you need it.

BASIC EQUIPMENT NEEDS

Forever collecting new gadgets to cram into a supersized shiny backpack, the equipment freak is happiest plunking down dollars in the friendly mountaineering shop. On the other hand, the purist buys a few pieces of recycled gear from the Goodwill and hangs them over a shoulder on a bit of frayed rope. Somewhere in between is the person who is neither extravagant nor spartan, the practical individual who knows the difference between wants and needs, between asceticism and extravagance. This is the Wise Backpacker, the WB.

The WB knows some basic equipment is necessary—clothing, food and water, shelter, sleeping gear, navigational aids, emergency items—and realizes some of this must come from the mountaineering shop. But the WB also knows some can be borrowed, rented, or picked up at bargain rates in surplus stores and at garage sales. The WB checks bulletin boards in outdooring shops, supermarkets, schools, and community centers; watches newspaper classified ads; keeps eyes and ears open when with outdooring friends, knowing full well that there is always someone who has equipment to sell or trade.

The WB avoids overkill, such as acquiring an Arctic expedition tent for sleeping in the backwoods of Alabama. The WB carries enough clothing, food, fuel, matches, and toilet paper to be safe and comfortable, allowing a little more for unexpected situations. The WB minimizes bulk and weight by avoiding canned foods, getting rid of unnecessary packaging, paring down frivolities, loading all gear compactly.

Speaking of weight, there are several rules of thumb for deciding the total weight a hiker can or should tote. One advises beginners to carry approximately one fourth the body weight for a man, one fifth the body weight for a woman. Another recommends that an experienced male carry around 50 pounds, a female about 30 pounds.

Rough guides, to be sure. I've known delicate-appearing women who could comfortably pack 50 pounds up hill and down dale, and wiry men who were quite happy hiking all day under an 85-pound load. It all depends on your body structure, your strength, and your mental attitude.

To find out what weight is best for you, initially load your pack with everything you think you'll need. Hoist it onto your shoulders and walk around the house. Walk around outside. If the pack feels comfortable and you think you can live with it for several hours a day, some of which may be uphill hiking, okay. But if instead of walking you lurch, caroming off walls and furniture, you'd better pare back the load.

The following chart is a typical backpacker's basic equipment checklist. Excluding food, it suggests items for an average person's average needs over an average period of time in an average backcountry during an average season of fair weather.

At home, don your fully loaded pack to check for balance and weight. If you need help getting in and out of it, you're probably carrying too much for the trail.

Don't feel you must follow this checklist slavishly, since you may not be average. Utilize it merely as a guide in gearing up, subtracting or adding whatever seems right for you. All items are discussed in detail in later chapters.

BASIC EQUIPMENT CHECKLIST

(Starred items are optional, or may be needed for special conditions)

Clothing

Hiking shoes

2 pair wool socks

2 pair thin inner socks

Thin shirt

Wool shirt

2 pair trousers

Belt or suspenders

Hat with brim, or cap

Rain gear

Windbreaker jacket

2 bandannas

*Underwear or T-shirt

*Wool stocking hat or balaclava

*Pair of mitten shells (or gloves)

*2 pair wool mitten liners

*Gaiters (short or long)

*Sneakers or moccasins

*Long underwear

*Hiking shorts

*Down jacket or down vest

*Extra shoelaces

Shelter and Bedding

Tarp or tent, with poles, stakes, lines

Ground cloth (groundsheet)

Sleeping pad

Sleeping bag in its own stuff sack

*Bivouac sack

Kitchen

Stove, with fuel

Wire pricker for stove orifice

Spare fuel

Cookware (two nesting pots, cup)

Pocketknife (Swiss Army type)

Spoon

Water bottle or canteen

Matches

*Eye dropper (for priming liquid-fuel stove)

*Plastic water bag

*Pot scrubber

*Ensolite square for stove

*Salt and pepper

Hygiene

Stuff sack, containing:

Toothbrush

Dentifrice

Deodorant

Small towel or washcloth

*Dental floss

*Soap

*Moist cleansing pads

*Extra toilet paper

Repair

Stuff sack, containing:
Fabric mending tape
Small pliers
4 feet of stranded wire

Sewing kit
Extra parts for pack frame
(clevis pins, split rings)
*Crampon wrench

Miscellaneous

Backpack
Day pack
Backpack rain cover
Insect repellent
Pencil
Note pad
1 or 2 extra stuff sacks (always come in handy)
2 or 3 plastic bags (for carry-out trash)
Sunglasses or dark goggles

Lip-balm stick (keep in windbreaker
pocket)
Toilet paper
*Hiking staff
*Paperback book
*Watch
*Spare eyeglasses
*Sun face cream
*Sun lip cream

Essentials (see details later in this chapter)

Stuff sack, containing:
Map of area
Compass
Extra food
Filled water bottle
Extra clothing

Flashlight, with extra bulb and batteries
Matches
Fire starter
Pocketknife
First-aid kit

BASIC WATER NEEDS

"A near tragedy," mused W. C. Fields. "The first week out on the expedition someone lost the bottle opener, and for the rest of the trip we had to subsist on food and water."

If you're in good health, missing a few meals is no tragedy; without food you can survive for many days, even weeks. However, without water or other fluids you won't last long at all.

Because the human body is approximately 80 percent fluids, constant liquid intake is absolutely essential to the normal functioning of the vital organs. When intake is exceeded by loss—through the natural processes of perspiration, urination, and exhalation—dehydration occurs. Slight dehydration can be tolerated for a short period of time, but when dehydration exceeds 6 to 8 percent of body weight, decreased efficiency will result. Uncorrected dehydration can end in complete collapse.

When backpacking, how much liquid does your body need? A minimum of two quarts a day if you're not exerting yourself, at least twice as much if

Safe and plentiful water is vital. Drinking from a high-altitude glacial stream is one of life's greatest joys, but if you have any doubts about the condition of the water, treat it with purifying compounds.

Even if you don't feel thirsty, drink plenty of liquids. Dehydration can cause numerous ailments.

you're working hard or the weather is hot. The best indication for drinking is thirst, and the best rule for drinking is *drink often.* There's no such thing as drinking too much water. If you feel the need to take a leak only infrequently, and your urine is dark in color and strong in smell, you're not taking in enough fluids.

Speaking practically, you can't carry much more than about two gallons of water, which means that if your backpacking trip is to last any longer than a day, you're going to have to obtain more water from natural sources, such as springs, streams, rivers, or lakes. In regions heavily trafficked by human beings, suspect all water, whatever its source. Though water may look crystal clear, smell pure, and taste good, it can be loaded with microscopic creatures that may not drop you on the spot but that can make you very sick later on.

Boiling water for five minutes will destroy most harmful organisms, and this you may do in the course of meal preparation anyway. But boiling water to fill a canteen is time-consuming and uses precious fuel. Perhaps the simplest way to treat doubtful water is with purifying tablets. Here you have a choice of chlorine-releasing compounds or iodine-releasing compounds, either of them obtainable in the form of a small pill that you drop into a given volume of water.

You shake the container, then let it stand for a few minutes to allow the chlorine or iodine to do its job, after which the water is safe to drink.

Chlorine compounds kill some harmful organisms, but iodine kills virtually all. So to be on the safe side, stick with iodine. You can disguise the taste by adding powdered fruit juice mix to the water *after* purification. Adding it before may inhibit the chemical action.

Of course, when it comes right down to a survival situation you'll thankfully drink whatever water you can find, no matter how unsavory it looks, smells, or tastes.

BASIC NUTRITION NEEDS

In regard to nutrition, a calorie is a measure of the energy value of foods. Without energy, as you may have found out around home, you don't accomplish very much. Therefore, to keep going as a backpacker you must consume foods that yield certain energy values. That is, you must provide your body with certain amounts of calories.

How many calories? That depends on many factors, such as your body structure, the degree of your physical activity, the altitude at which you hike, the temperature, and so on. The average backpacker needs from 2,500 calories a day for moderately easy summer hiking to 5,000 calories a day (or more) for rigorous cold-weather mountaineering.

To take in the proper amount of calories, you must eat foods containing proper amounts of carbohydrates, proteins, and fats.

Carbohydrates

Carbohydrates are compounds that include starches, sugars, and cellulose. Easily digested, carbohydrates are absorbed into the blood and delivered as "simple sugars" to the body's cells, where they combine with oxygen to produce bursts of energy. However, since the body doesn't store carbohydrates for future use, they must be replenished if energy needs continue. Breakfasts, lunches, and trail snacks should be heavy in carbohydrates to supply energy throughout the day; most nutritionists recommend that at least 50 percent of one's calorie requirements be in the form of carbohydrates.

Bakery goods are a fine source of carbohydrates. Some of the handiest bakery goods for backpacking include pumpernickel bread, cocktail rye, pilot crackers, and graham crackers.

Most cereals are high in carbohydrates: instant oatmeal and farina, granola, and *muesli* (a Swiss concoction). For backpacking, avoid cereals that require long cooking; the kinds that merely mix in hot or cold water take less time to prepare and leave less of a mess to clean up. They also require less fuel. For an extra taste treat, or as a nutrition extra, add brown sugar, nuts, and raisins or other dried fruits.

Pasta, rice, and potatoes are also carbohydrate-rich foods. Quickest cooking of any of the pastas is *ramen,* an Asian noodle to which you simply add hot water. Many brands of ramen come with a packet of tasty seasoning. Like other backpacking cereals, rice should be the quick-cooking kind for ease of preparation. "Instant" rice dinners are available in such flavors as chicken, beef, curry, and tomato. Instant mashed potatoes reconstitute in a jiffy and can be jazzed up with gravies or sauces, dried onions, dried mushrooms, or whatever else pleases your palate.

Fruits (a good source of carbohydrates and simple sugar) add a nice taste touch to any meal or snack. Supermarket dried fruits—such as raisins, peaches, apricots, apples, pears, prunes, bananas, and figs—weigh more than freeze-dried varieties, but they cost less.

Sugar, properly known as sucrose, is a quick-energy food that satisfies one's sweet tooth. Use brown or granulated sugar in cereal, coffee, tea, or other drinks. Candy bars and hard candies are chiefly sucrose and so make good trail munchies.

Proteins

Proteins are organic compounds that are broken down by digestion into amino acids, which are essential in the release of food energy and necessary in the building of body tissues. The adult human body manufactures some—but not all—proteins that are required for building materials. Therefore, to provide the materials needed, you must consume protein. Proteins are digested slowly, and the energy they provide is released slowly. Therefore, protein-rich foods are best eaten for the last meal of the day so the body can work on them while it's resting. About 25 percent of your calorie intake should be in the form of proteins.

Complete proteins contain the essential amino acids, those the human body needs but can't make. Most complete proteins come from animals: for example, meat, cheese, eggs, and milk. But nonmeat eaters take heart. Incomplete proteins (from plants, such as cereals and legumes) can be complemented with the addition of milk, eggs, or cheese.

Canned meats, including chipped beef, chicken, turkey, sardines, herring, and tuna are fairly rich in protein and easily carried. (Be sure to carry out the empty container!) Beef jerky and salami are protein-rich and make good snacks.

Cheese is an excellent protein food that can be eaten by itself or combined with almost anything. But be aware that "processed cheese foods" may not contain cheese at all, and they do not keep well beyond a couple of days.

Dried whole eggs can be prepared by themselves or mixed with other foods, and nonfat dry milk can be combined with almost anything.

Some other high-protein foods include peanut butter, wheat germ, nuts, and soybeans (one of the highest).

Fats

The most concentrated energy source of all (though they also contribute to the manufacture of building materials), fats take considerable time to digest. For this reason, fatty foods should be consumed in small quantities. Approximately 25 percent of your calorie intake should be in the form of fats.

Bacon (canned or bar) is a good fat source, as are cheddar cheeses, chocolate, nuts, and margarine (so is butter, but without refrigeration it doesn't keep as well as margarine).

Relative Energy Values

The following table gives a very rough comparison of the relative energy values of certain groups of backpacking foods.

FOOD	ENERGY VALUE		
	Carbohydrates	Proteins	Fats
Dairy products	Moderately low	Moderate	Moderate
Meat and fish	Moderately high	High	Moderate
Grains, cereals, and pastas	High	High	Insignificant
Fruits and fruit juices	Moderate	Moderately low	Insignificant
Nuts	Moderately high	Moderately high	High
Vegetables	High	Moderately high	Insignificant
Baked goods	High	Moderately high	Moderate
Candies and sweets	Moderately high	Moderately low	Moderately high

One of the most heartrending lamentations heard on a backpacking trip is, "But I thought *you* had it!" Especially when "it" refers to a first-aid item. Whether hiking alone or traveling in a group, every backpacker should have a first-aid kit. Don't count on your companions for extra aspirin or moleskin. They may be counting on you for it.

Ready-made first-aid kits may be fine in the car or at home, where professional aid is but a phone call away, but they never seem quite right for outdooring needs. Usually the store-bought kit has too much of this or too little of that for the backpacker. Assembling your own kit is neither time-consuming nor costly, and when you put it together yourself you know exactly what's in it and where.

Everyone has a personal preference for the contents of the first-aid kit. The following basic list assumes an average trek over average terrain in average weather. More rigorous efforts may call for additional items.

Dressings
  20 adhesive bandages (such as Band-Aids)—for small wounds
   6 butterfly strips—for closing large cuts
   4 each, 2×2-inch and 4×4-inch gauze squares—for large wounds
   1 roll of 1-inch-wide adhesive tape—to hold dressings in place
   1 2-inch elastic bandage—for sprained ankle or knee

Drugs and Medications
  20 aspirin tablets—to relieve mild pain
  10 codeine tablets (prescription required)—for severe pain
  20 Lomotil tablets (prescription required)—for diarrhea
  24 salt tablets (or powdered "athlete's drink")—to help prevent heat exhaustion
  Tube of antibiotic ointment (prescription required)—for minor wounds
  Personal medications as needed

Miscellaneous
  Needles and safety pins—for removing splinters, securing dressings
  Tweezers—for removing splinters
  Scissors—for cutting bandages
  Single-edge razor blade—for cutting bandages, shaving hair

Moleskin—for blister prevention
Antibacterial soap—for cleansing wounds
First-aid manual—for on-the-spot directions

Pack all first-aid items snugly in a sturdy plastic or aluminum container. Before every trip check the contents to make certain nothing has gone astray and to see if anything needs replenishing. Don't wait until you're three days away from a drugstore to learn you're out of moleskin.

THE ESSENTIALS KIT

Way back when, before backpacking became the tremendously popular sport it now is, many veteran outdoors people carried in a corner of their pack a small collection of items they dubbed emergency gear. These bits and pieces were for use only in a survival situation. I don't know when such extras came to be collectively called "essentials," or who first put them together in kit form, but the name, as well as the function, is highly appropriate to today's backpacker.

In an emergency the following essential items could save your life. Keep them together in a small stuff sack *in your day pack,* so they will always be with you, even on short forays out of camp. Never leave them behind in your tent or backpack.

1. Map of area. A topographic map is your guide; without it you could become hopelessly lost.

2. Compass. Together with a map, a compass can be your salvation. Make sure you know how to use it (see chapter 5).

3. Extra food. This is food that should not be touched except in an emergency, food that will keep for a long period. It needn't be especially appetizing but should be highly nutritious. For example: pemmican, high-energy fruit bars, meat bars.

4. Filled water bottle. Any time you leave camp, make sure you carry water. Dehydration can weaken the body fast.

5. Extra clothing. An emergency may keep you out all night, so make sure you can stay warm and dry. Wherever I go, an extra sweater, lightweight rain pants, and a rain jacket go with me.

6. Sunglasses or dark goggles. Bright sun can be destructive to the eyes, especially over snow or at high altitudes. Protect your eyes.

7. Flashlight, with extra bulb and batteries. Walking in the dark is risky business. A flashlight, with spare bulb and extra batteries, is a must.

8. Matches. These are extra matches, separate from your normal supply. Use wooden matches in a sealed container, backpacker's waterproofed matches, or book matches wrapped securely in plastic.

9. Fire starter. Starting a fire with soggy kindling requires a steady flame for several minutes. One match can start a candle stub or fuel tablet, which will then bring damp kindling to combustion.

10. Pocketknife. Perhaps the backpacker's most versatile tool, a pocketknife can be used in first aid, food preparation, fire starting, and so on. In addition to carrying a knife in your pocket, carry a spare in your essentials kit.

11. First-aid kit. Make up a kit from the list given earlier in this chapter, and know how to use everything in it.

To these basics you can add items to suit your own fancy or fulfill your own needs. My essentials kit includes a small spool of monofilament line and some fishhooks. In addition to its obvious function, the line could be used to construct a small-animal snare. I also carry 50 feet of braided nylon cord, which has a variety of uses ranging from equipment repairs to hanging food out of bears' reach. Persons allergic to bee stings should carry antivenin. Some people swear by a "space blanket." Though never having needed one for myself, I once wrapped an accident victim in a space blanket prior to evacuation. It helped conserve body heat.

Garbing and Clothing

Primitive folks may have padded around on their bare feet over sharp rocks and hot sand, but you —being a member of a civilized, affluent society— are more likely than not to wear shoes outdoors. What kind of shoes depends on where you'll be planting your feet and when.

ABOUT FOOTWEAR

For that summer day hike, or even on an overnight jaunt along a good trail, some hikers prefer the light weight and flexibility of sneakers, tennis shoes, deck shoes, or other fabric-and-rubber footwear. Such shoes are fine for short strolls on a dry, beaten track, where there aren't a lot of sticks and stones and ruts to bruise tender feet. Though the next best thing to walking barefoot on a nice day, they are next to worthless in bad weather or on lumpy ground. (The young woman I once observed flip-flopping along the trail in spongy thongs was, I thought, carrying things a bit too far.)

On longer, rougher treks your feet are going to want something more substantial than mere fabric and rubber. With your body mass balanced

63

For young and old alike, good hiking shoes are a must if you plan any type of extended trekking.

on them, plus that of a pack, mile after mile, you'd best baby your feet with lightweight or medium-weight trail boots. Designed primarily for trail hiking with a pack, or hiking over somewhat rough terrain, lightweight and medium-weight trail boots have flexible or semiflexible uppers and soles, as well as high ankle support.

Mountaineering boots are designed for off-trail slogging with a heavy pack, over rugged terrain and snow. Though normally too stiff for summer or trail wear, mountaineering boots are worn by a few hikers who either over-buy or who like heavy-duty protection year-round. The stiff leather and heavy construction of mountaineering boots give excellent foot and ankle support, and a steel or plastic shank embedded in the midsole ensures the kind of rigidness necessary for crampon use.

Expedition or cold-weather mountaineering boots are designed for high-altitude climbing in subzero temperatures. They have very sturdy reinforced uppers, thick padding around the tongue, and a strong midsole shank; some even have an inner boot of felt or soft leather for added insulation. Definitely overkill for all but the fiercest situations.

Let's sum up the type of shoe for the type of hiking, with their average weights (women's sizes may weigh somewhat less):

- For day walks or short strolls on good trails: sneakers, tennis shoes, deck shoes, or other lightweight footwear. Weight: 1 to 1½ pounds each.
- For long trail hiking with a pack, or for trekking over rough ground: medium-weight fabric shoes or medium-weight trail boots. Weight: 1½ to 3 pounds each.
- For cross-country excursions with a heavy pack or for glacier travel: mountaineering boots. Weight: 2 to 5 pounds each.
- For high-altitude climbing in cold weather: mountaineering or expedition boots: Weight: 5 to 8 pounds each.

Almost all hiking and mountaineering boots have lug or cleated outsoles (the part that comes in contact with the ground). Though some strongly conservation-minded backpackers consider them damaging to the environment, lug soles grip well on almost any surface and so are the sport's standard underpinning. One exception is the good old common work boot, sold across the country by Sears, Roebuck, J. C. Penney, Montgomery Ward, and many department stores. Relatively inexpensive, durable, and adequate for most dry-weather hiking, work boots have a flexible crepe sole, a soft upper, and a high top. Some outdoors folks wouldn't be caught dead wearing them, but quite a few old trail hands swear by them.

Climbing shoes are designed for technical rock climbing, not for hiking.

A

B

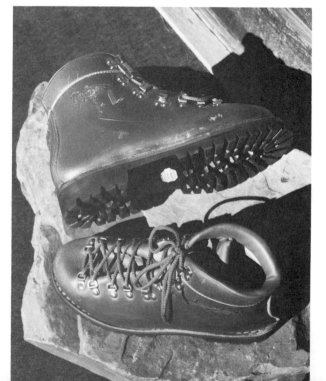

Lightweight shoes (A), designed for beaten-path hiking and light load carrying, are flexible and have patterned soles. Medium-weight shoes, or trail boots (B), are designed for trekking over rough terrain. They provide some ankle support and often have lug soles. Mountaineering, or expedition, boots (C) have heavy, rigid soles, solid toes for kicking steps in snow, and interior padding for comfort and insulation.

C

Thin and lightweight, they have either a soft, smooth sole (fine for steep granite, hazardous on grass and loose soil) or a stiff lug sole for edging, soft uppers, and a rubber strip around the lower part of the shoe for friction in cracks. Some climbing shoes are torsionally rigid and so give good support for standing on very narrow ledges. Others are flexible, permitting the foot to be twisted into tortuous forms understandable only to a climber.

I've heard of hikers wearing moccasins for trail tramping ("Almost as good as bare feet," some claim), but I have yet to see one so shod. Because moccasins offer the foot no support and little protection, they are bad news for backpackers. Yet their glovelike squishiness does feel delightful around camp after you've shucked off your hiking boots. Other "relaxing" shoes that are easy on trail-tender feet include sneakers and down booties.

Choosing Shoes

The time has come when you've decided your threadbare sneakers can no longer support your sagging arches, and you're determined to take the plunge. You walk into a well-stocked outdooring store and sidle nervously into the shoe department. As you gaze about in wonderment, your mind boggles at the variety in types of outdooring footwear, in shapes, styles, and brands, and in cost.

Cost is the real killer. For one pair of hiking shoes you may pay two to five times what you'd lay out for street shoes. But remember that your hiking shoes are probably the most important purchase you'll make in outdooring gear, so choose carefully and be prepared to spend a few bucks. If your feet aren't happy in the backcountry, you won't go anywhere.

First, what are your needs? What kind of hiking over what kind of terrain will you be doing? If day hikes and occasional weekenders on well-traveled, even trails are your only goals, you might as well stick with tennis shoes. If you expect to tramp frequently on beaten tracks, straying into the bush once in a while, consider a good light- or medium-weight trail shoe. If your pleasure is bushwacking on cross-country slogs lasting several days, go for a heavy-weight boot.

Tell the store clerk your needs, have your feet measured for size, and ask to see several styles in the kind of shoe you're after. While the clerk is fetching them, slip a pair of heavy wool socks over your everyday socks. A good store will provide them for fitting.

Get one shoe on but don't lace it. Now slide your foot all the way forward and poke an index finger down behind your heel. If that finger won't slip down,

In one day, backpacking may take you from worn trail to jagged rock, so anticipate the most severe terrain and choose your hiking shoes accordingly.

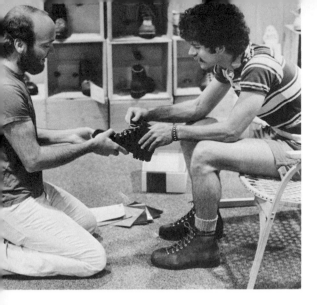

When buying shoes, discuss your needs with a knowledgeable sales clerk. Try on different styles or makes to find the most comfortable fit.

With your foot all the way forward in an unlaced shoe, you should be able to easily slide a finger down behind your heel. If you can't, the shoes are probably too small. If there's a lot of space around the finger, the shoes are too large.

the shoes are too small. If there's a lot of space around it, they are too big. If you touch the shoe sole and the back of your heel, you're on the way to a proper fit.

Now put both shoes on and, while sitting, kick the heels against the floor until your own heels are all the way back in them. Lace the shoes snugly and walk around. If the store has a sloping surface, such as the front of a fitting stool, stand flatfooted on it, first with toes pointed downward, then with toes pointed upward. Do your feet slop around or slide forward in the shoes? If so, try a smaller size. Do your feet seem cramped or your toes overly confined? Try a larger size. Your toes should not bunch up, nor should your heels lift inside the shoes. Generally, a hiking shoe should be generous in length, snug in width.

Even within the same size by the same manufacturer there may be slight differences. Try on several pairs of shoes until you find *the* pair, the one pair that encloses your feet lovingly. Shoes must feel comfortable. If they don't, something is wrong. If you can't get a good fit in one store, go to another.

Buying shoes by mail order is tricky business, as it usually involves sending off a tracing of your stockinged foot (the bigger one). To ensure a good fit, follow the supplier's instructions carefully. When the shoes arrive, don them and walk around indoors several times over a couple of days. If they don't feel right on your feet, return them for an exchange.

As you inspect shoes, take your time, weigh all the factors, and enlist the help of a knowledgeable salesperson. Check the following detailing. Your final choice between two models may hinge on the way the laces work or how the sole attaches.

Weight

Trail boots top the scales around 3 pounds each; over 5 and you're into heavy-weight or expedition boots. Since you're going to be picking your feet up and laying them down, mile after mile, mind the weight on them. Everything else being equal between two models, pick the lighter boot or shoe.

Outer Skin

The leather of hiking boots is either rough-side-out or smooth-side-out. This means their exterior is either suedelike or slick-looking. Rough-side-out seems to wear longer; both can be made water-repellent. Choose whichever pleases you more.

Sole Construction

Most outdooring shoes have neoprene-lug soles designed to provide good friction on steep surfaces. One-piece molded lug soles usually are not replaceable. When they wear out, you have to chuck the entire shoe, even though the upper is still in good shape. Most separate sole-and-heel configurations can be replaced at a cost one fourth to one third that of the original shoe. Not cheap, but better than starting all over again.

The soles of lesser-known shoe brands may vary in color from yellow to brown to gray. Such lighter hues indicate a low carbon content, which means the soles are far less durable than darker ones.

Sole Attachment

The boot you inspect may have one or more rows of visible stitching where the upper fastens to the midsole. Generally, three rows of stitching are stronger than two, two are stronger than one. If no stitches show, they may be inside, or the sole may be fastened by a process called injection molding. Either system is acceptable.

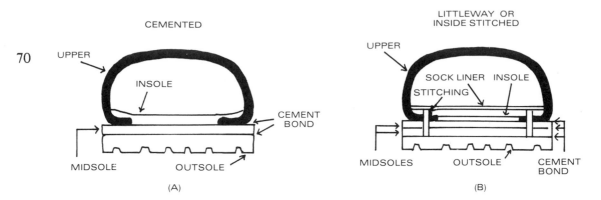

Most hiking boot soles are attached to uppers by one of four principal methods. Cemented boots (A) have a one-piece lug sole glued to the leather of the upper, which is folded under a light insole; cemented soles have no stitching and give little support. Littleway, or inside stitched, boots (B) have the upper leather sandwiched between the insole and one or more midsoles; the inside stitching enables the sole to be trimmed very close, a desirable feature for climbing shoes. The Goodyear

Lacing

For lacing, shoes may have metal eyelets, flat hooks, rings, or various combinations of these. Hooks are quicker to lace and unlace than eyelets or rings, but they should run only from about the ankle on up. Any lower and they have a tendency to snag grasses or be smashed shut by contact with rocks. If a lacing fixture ever breaks, it can be replaced by a good shoe-repair shop.

Closure

Ideally, a shoe tongue should have some form of side attachment (such as stitching, or soft leather flaps called gussets) to keep it from shifting and to prevent seeds, stickers, and other foreign matter from working their way inside. Sturdier boots may have a series of flaps that close over the tongue. They're a bit stiff but are a virtual guarantee that nothing (including water) will get in. For comfort's sake, as well as for a better fit, tongues should be padded above the instep.

Lining and Padding

The least-expensive and lightest-weight boots have a single layer of leather enclosing the upper part of the foot. However, most hikers prefer the comfort of a lined boot, which has a smooth inside layer of leather, or else a padded boot, which has rubber or foam between inside and outside leather layers. Padded "scree collars" around the top feel good—especially when you're breaking in new boots—but they are only marginally effective at keeping out loose stuff such as small pebbles.

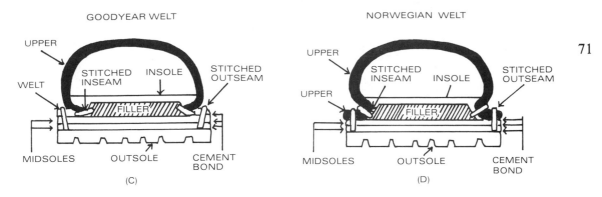

welt process (C) involves the upper, which is stitched directly to the insole, and the outsole, midsole, and welt, which are stitched together; such boots give good foot protection and support when hiking with a heavy load. Norwegian welt boots (D) have two or three rows of heavy stitching along the ledge where upper and sole meet, resulting in an extremely rugged boot.

Break-in and Care

It's a moot point whether shoes are broken in or feet are broken down. Whichever, a fitting marriage must be performed and a happy honeymoon consummated if shoes and feet are to be compatible ever after. Fabric shoes need little or no breaking in. However, much lore and twaddle exist in regard to breaking in leather boots, there being as many schools of thought as there are styles from which to choose. Though a few of the methods seem to border on black magic, each appears to work in its own way for some people.

Basic to all breaking-in methods is wearing new boots indoors for three or four days. If your feet slip around or feel horribly scrunched, exchange the boots for a better fit and wear those indoors for a while. Most stores will take boots back as long as they haven't been worn outdoors.

If, indoors, your feet feel you've made a good choice, wear the boots on short hikes. First try strolling for a couple of hours on level ground, then graduate to a half-day walk with a little uphill thrown in for variety. To prevent heel blisters—the most common curse of breaking in boots—use one-inch adhesive tape or moleskin on your heels (see "Caring for Your Feet" later in this chapter). After a few take-it-easy hikes over a week or two, your feet and boots will accept each other.

A more drastic method of breaking in boots involves filling them with hot water. That's right, hot (not boiling) water! After a minute, empty the boots and lace your feet securely into them, wearing socks you expect to wear hiking. Now walk outdoors for half a day, or until you think things are dry, at which time the leather should be softened and conformed to your feet. What the hot-water treatment does is simulate in a short time what your perspiration does over a longer period.

Despite all precautions, your feet may sprout a lovely crop of blisters during the breaking-in process, but better blisters at home than miles out on the trail. Always break in new boots long *before* a hike, and don't start a hike until blisters are healed.

You'll often hear and read about "waterproofing" hiking boots, but the term is a misnomer. Truly waterproof footwear is made of impermeable rubber or plastic, and those boots ain't made for walkin'. Leather is porous stuff, ideal for encasing feet, which need to "breathe." Sealing hiking boots totally may keep water out, but your feet will simmer in their own juices, and the leather will stew right along with them. Hiking boots should be made *water repellent,* which means most water will run off their surface.

To make boots water repellent—and, more important, to guard against their drying out and stiffening like giant cornflakes—you must periodically treat them, before they become wet, with a liquid, paste, or spray-on conditioning compound. Which you use depends on how the leather was treated at the time the boots were made.

When you buy boots, find out from the clerk or from the manufacturer's literature whether the leather was chrome-tanned or oil-tanned. Oil-tanned (also called vegetable-tanned) leather takes oil or boot grease; chrome-tanned leather takes a silicone wax. A boot that is combination-tanned should be treated with a silicone wax.

Any time your boots become wet, let them dry out slowly and completely, then apply a conditioning compound. For oil-tanned leather, apply oil or grease liberally, rubbing it in at the juncture of sole and upper (called the welt). Let the boots stand for several hours in a warm, well-ventilated place so the compound can penetrate the leather. For chrome-tanned leather, use silicone wax. Spray or brush on a liquid, or rub in a paste, making sure plenty of it soaks into the welt and seams, where water first enters the boot.

Never use oil or grease on chrome-tanned leather. It fills the pores so that the boots, and your feet, can't breathe. In sealing a boot's welt, try to keep all compounds away from the sole edges, as the compounds may dissolve the glues used to bond together the sole layers.

In your zeal to take care of your boots, don't overdo the conditioning treatment. Boots should be treated only once or twice a year, or when they seem dried out.

The worst enemy of leather is heat, and the best way to murder boots is

Wet shoes should be dried and aired upside down as long as possible, away from fire and hot, direct sun.

to broil them next to a campfire or in hot sun. When boots are wet on a trek, let them air out away from fires as long as possible. They may still be clammy when you get into them, but grin and bear it. If boots are wet by the time you get home, wipe them with a damp cloth, stuff them with crumpled newspaper, and stand them in an airy place. When they've dried thoroughly, brush off caked mud. A whitish deposit on the leather usually means it's drying out and needs re-treatment.

Socks and Such

Every hiker has his or her own quirk about how many and what kind of socks to wear. Some advocate a single pair of heavy wool socks, others swear by two sets of woolies, and so on. What seems to be the most widely accepted practice is to wear a pair of thin inner socks (synthetic, or wool and synthetic blend) and a pair of heavy wool socks over them. This combination seems to give good insulation, pads the feet nicely, and minimizes blistering. If some other system makes your feet happier, so be it.

For a little more padding and insulation, you might want to slip a pair of insoles into your boots. And if weak arches give you trouble, add a set of store-bought or custom-made arch supports. Remember to remove such gadgets when drying wet boots, to prevent the growth of mold.

On a bitterly cold winter hike a few years ago, someone recommended wearing thin plastic bags—the kind you pick up in supermarket produce departments—to keep my feet warmer. Game to try anything once, I slithered stockinged feet into plastic bags, then into my boots. It worked! My feet sweated like a pair of racehorses, but in subzero temperatures they stayed toasty warm. To avoid having your feet slip around in your boots, wear the plastic bags between sock layers, not next to your skin.

One or two thin inner socks plus a heavy wool sock will minimize foot blisters. Put on clean inner socks daily.

Caring for Your Feet

Armies may travel on their stomachs, but backpackers travel on their feet. If backpacking feet aren't given loving care, they'll let their owner know about it before many miles. A careless novice hiker isn't called tenderfoot for nothing.

Foot care begins at home. First comes properly fitted and properly broken-in boots, as we talked about earlier in this chapter. Then comes attention to your feet *before* you hit the trail. Bothersome corns, bunions, or ingrown toenails should be taken care of by a podiatrist or chiropodist at least a week ahead of a trip. Toenails should be trimmed a couple of days before heading out, not the same day.

An old Army trick for pampering tender feet is to coat them liberally with shaving cream before donning socks. As you walk, your feet may feel squishy, but it's the slipperiness that defeats friction and so prevents blisters from developing. Use shaving *cream* rather than foam, which evaporates and is absorbed too fast. The mentholated variety smells fresh and feels cool.

If you hike a lot your feet probably won't trouble you, but if you're a once-in-a-while backpacker you may have to baby them a little each time. Feet do get tired. After all, they carry not only your body weight but also the mass of everything on your back. When you take a lunch break, loosen your shoe-laces and wiggle your toes. However, be wary of undressing your feet for too long. Freeing them may feel so grand you'll be reluctant to tug your shoes back on. In camp, padding around in a softer, loose kind of shoe—such as sneakers —allows weary feet to spread comfortably and smile contentedly.

As you hike, be alert to any messages your feet may send you. Tenderness on the bottoms may indicate the need for arch supports. (You can find ready-made supports in the foot-care section of drugstores or variety stores, or you can have a podiatrist make up a set, but the latter will cost at least ten times as much as the former.) An allover aching feeling below the ankles means you've probably gone far enough for one day. A localized burning or "hot spot," especially on the heels, means friction is building a blister. That's the sign to stop immediately and protect the sore place. Try to put up with a hot spot, and you may be sorry.

Moleskin is the old standby for keeping hot spots from developing into blisters. Available in drugstores, it's a fluffy, feltlike material with an adhesive backing, and it comes in postcard-size pieces or in large sheets. Mole*foam* is similar, only thicker and more padded. To use either, cut a rectangular piece somewhat larger than the irritated area, rounding the corners to keep them from working loose under your sock. Peel the plastic backing off and lay the piece right on the hot spot, rubbing out from the middle to make it adhere all over. Now when you walk, the hot spot won't receive any more friction and —if you've caught it in time—a blister won't form.

When a hot spot goes beyond the burning stage and begins to hurt, you've got a proper blister. Though it can give you the miseries, a blister isn't likely

To guard against blisters, apply a large piece of moleskin or molefoam before starting to hike or as soon as you feel a "hot spot." Trim the corners to prevent the dressing from peeling off.

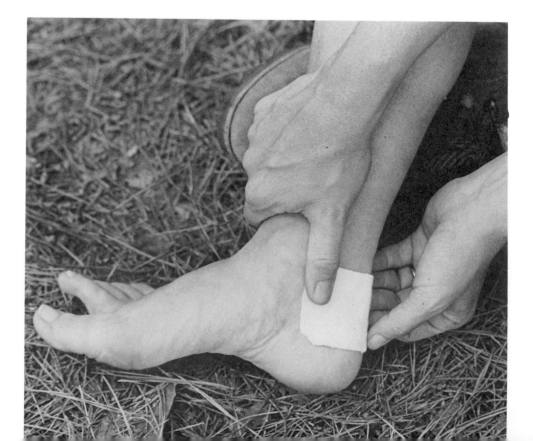

to lay you low as long as you treat it promptly. If it's small and flat, just cover it with moleskin as you would a hot spot. I have a friend who cuts a hole in the moleskin so it surrounds a small blister rather than covering it over.

A puffy, fluid-filled blister needs more attention. Cleanse the area thoroughly, then sterilize a needle or the tip of a sharp knife blade by holding it for a second in a flame. Puncture the edge of the blister and gently press to remove the fluid, then wipe the area clean again. Put on a piece of sterile gauze and cover that with moleskin. Change the dressing occasionally and keep your feet clean, to avoid infection.

ABOUT CLOTHING

Whenever I contemplate jamming an extra article of clothing into an already overloaded pack, my mind flashes back to the trouserless hiker I once encountered in the Cascades. And I don't mean he was wearing undershorts. Just shoes, socks, T-shirt, and a backpack. Swinging along the trail, he seemed happy as a lark, despite an autumn nip to the morning. After we exchanged pleasantries he explained he seldom wore pants in the backcountry. According to him, pants added weight, whether in the pack or on the body. Besides, he liked the open air.

Though it makes an interesting picture, and might save on weight, I hesitate suggesting that hikers travel in the buff. Never can tell who you might meet.

On the other hand, backpacking does not require that you be decked out in sartorial elegance, popular-magazine hype notwithstanding. For serious outdoors people, backpacking isn't a fashion-plate activity, and most dedicated trekkers care little about their appearance. Some old trail hands even delight in wearing the most raggle-taggle garb they can gather, flouting the chic that has taken over most sports.

The point is, looks are not important, whereas comfort and protection are. That pair of hip-hugging trousers may look sharp, but it restricts movement and impedes blood circulation. That flimsy blouse may appear fetching around home, but in the woods it's little barrier to mosquitoes and no retainer of body heat.

Basic Needs

As with most backpacking items, you should learn to distinguish needs from desires. Pack what you need; then, if there's any room left, and if you're willing to put up with extra weight and bulk, go ahead and yield to your desires. What are a backpacker's basic clothing needs? Let's look at the types of hikes considered in the previous chapter.

First comes the dry-weather, close-to-home day hike. Almost anything goes here, and almost everything you need can be worn right on your body: shoes, socks, pants or hiking shorts, a thin shirt. In your day pack you might include a lightweight sweater and a windbreaker, just in case the afternoon brings a cooling breeze.

For an overnight summer jaunt, in addition to the clothing for a day hike you should include an extra pair of pants (in case the other becomes soaked with rain or perspiration) as well as a long-sleeved, lightweight wool shirt. A hat or cap will keep your head warm or shield it from direct sun, and a poncho or rain suit will help keep you dry. Extra socks are a good idea.

Even for the long haul of a week or two, clothing remains pretty basic and strictly functional: hiking shoes, two pairs of thin socks, two pairs of heavy wool socks, a thin long-sleeved shirt, a wool long-sleeved shirt, two pairs of pants, a head covering, a bandanna or two, a windbreaker, rain gear, a sweater. Optional or seasonal items might include two sets of underwear, a stocking hat, mittens, gaiters, sneakers or moccasins, long underwear, a down or pile jacket, extra shoelaces.

Choices and Variations

Establishing your basic clothing needs is a fairly straightforward matter. Now let's take a look at some of the choices open to you, some of the specialized outdooring garb available to create variations on a theme.

Underwear

Backpackers who consider underwear unnecessary anywhere, any time, can skip the next few lines. But if that loose and easy feeling isn't for you, at least keep things simple. Females should leave delicate, lacy underthings at home and wear sturdy, practical items on the trail. Males should consider brief-style undershorts rather than the boxer variety, which tends to bunch uncomfortably on hot days. Synthetics or synthetic blends rinse out easily and dry quickly. For both men and women a synthetic-and-cotton T-shirt is a versatile bit of clothing. In dry weather it can be used as an underwear top, worn as a single shirt, or slipped on as a nightshirt.

Wide-weave fishnet underwear works on the theory of trapping pockets of insulating air in its "holes" when an outer garment is worn over it. With no outer garment, air can circulate freely, cooling the skin. Some hikers don't care for fishnet because backpack hip belts tend to grind the net into tender flesh.

For really cold weather, there is long woolen underwear, or underwear woven from synthetic materials. If the very thought of wool makes your skin itch, look for the soft, fluffy kind—expensive, but warm and nonscratchy. Or try the double-layer cotton-and-wool variety. Or wear the synthetics, though they tend to develop odors sooner than do natural fabrics.

Overwear

Trousers should be roomy both behind and below, otherwise you'll strain seams bending over a stream or hunkering up to a stove. (When fitting yourself, be sure to allow for shrinkage.) Leg bottoms should come over your boot tops, to keep out pebbles and such, but not be so long as to drag at your heels. Unless you enjoy collecting seeds, gravel, bugs, and other such goodies, wear cuffless trousers with straight legs. Wide-bottoms have more material than a weight-conscious backpacker needs, and all that floppy fabric is conducive to tripping over your own feet.

If you like the air-conditioned feeling of hiking shorts, wear them. But when your legs are bare be alert for wind chill, sunburn, stinging nettles, mosquitoes, scratchy brush, sharp-edged grasses, and poison sumac, ivy, or oak. If you encounter any or all of the above, just slip regular pants on over your shorts and continue on your way.

For some reason, knickers are more popular in Europe than in the United States. If you like knickers, wear ankle-length socks in warm weather and undo the pants below your knees for air circulation. When the weather turns cool, put on knee-length socks.

If air force blue, marine green, or army olive drab doesn't turn you off, you can find good pants buys in surplus stores. Sears, Ward's, and Penney's all have heavy-duty work pants that are dandy for outdooring.

A lightweight long-sleeved shirt is excellent sun and mosquito protection. If you get warm, unbutton the front all the way and let the bottom hang outside your pants for maximum ventilation. Turn the collar up to prevent a broiled neck. A no-iron, cotton-synthetic blend will dry fast while you're wearing it or when draped over a rock. However, a lightweight, woven wool shirt is worth the slight extra bulk. Worn over another shirt, a wool shirt provides warmth. One of the most popular items of backpacker garb is the "chamois" shirt, which

Warm-weather hiking means you can usually dress lightly, but no matter how nice the day, make sure you have warmer clothing in your pack. When hiking through brushlands or high grass, don long pants to protect your legs.

is soft, warm, and itch-free. But, being napped cotton, it will absorb moisture
like a sponge.

If your pack has plenty of carrying space and you anticipate really nasty weather, you might consider a sweater knit from raw wool. Because the natural oils have not been removed, the garment is somewhat water repellent. And if an oiled wool sweater does become soaked, you can squeeze most of the water out, put the sweater back on, and stay warm. Pullover sweaters are more efficient heat savers than the zipper or button-front type because they have no gaps for drafts to sneak through.

Outerwear

Wool keeps you warm because it traps dead air between its loose fibers, and that air is warmed by your own body heat. *Dead* air is the key. If a stiff wind comes up while you're snugged in wool, it will whistle right through the fibers, blowing away warm air and replacing it with cold. Your internal thermal machine works harder and harder to heat the air around your body, but because the warmed air is constantly being drawn away you never quite catch up. This is what's known as "getting cold."

To keep breezes and colder air from stealing warmth, you need something to block or break the wind. A nylon windbreaker or wind shell does just that. An extremely thin and lightweight jacket that reaches to the waist, it deflects wind, allowing your upper body to go about the business of keeping itself warm. For the legs there are wind pants that slip on over regular pants and work just like a jacket.

A different kind of windbreaker is the mountain parka, usually made of 60 percent nylon and 40 percent cotton, or sometimes of cotton and Dacron in a proportion of 65/35. So popular is this type of jacket that "60/40" has become its generic name, recognized by most outdoor-gear salespeople. The fabric is wind resistant and—in a very light drizzle—somewhat water repellent. However, don't expect a mountain parka to keep water out unless you treat it. I spray mine periodically with Thompson's Water Seal, a liquid used chiefly for sealing wood and concrete, then let it air for a couple of days.

Parkas reach below the hips, have a waist drawstring to shut out drafts, a hood, and a full-length zipper-and-snap closure in front.

An anorak is a fanny-length pullover (no closure) with a hood and, usually, a big kangaroo-pouch kind of pocket at belly height. Both hood and bottom have drawstrings. Anoraks made with uncoated fabric are intended for wind protection; coated fabrics repel water.

Rainwear

Like anoraks, cagoules are pullovers, only they reach all the way down to the knees and are water repellent. Cagoules are used chiefly by European rock climbers as bivouac bags. Donning a cagoule, you sit, bring your knees up to your chest, and tighten the bottom drawstring. Not very comfortable, but one way to weather out a storm. Because cagoules and anoraks have no front opening, any exertion turns them into sweat sacks.

Perhaps the most widely used piece of backpacking rain gear is the poncho. It's a rectangular sheet of water-repellent material (usually coated nylon) with a head hole and hood in the center and snaps along two sides. Two lengths are available. The regular one covers you but not your backpack, coming down to about your knees. The longer one covers you *and* your pack, giving you a

Rainwear can include any water-repellent gear, ranging from ponchos to jackets, from pants to plastic bags. Wear whatever keeps you dry.

deformed look. Side snaps allow you to make "sleeves" around your arms or to shorten the hanging-down part.

Ponchos do a good job of keeping most of your body dry if rain is falling straight down and the air is still. But if a wind kicks up they flap and billow like a torn sail. Then the best you can do is grab handfuls of material on both sides and pull it close, or stand out of the wind and wait for the storm to pass.

Some backpackers wear rain chaps or rain pants in addition to a poncho, thus remaining fairly dry even in heavy rain and high wind. Others don't mess around with a parka but get into rain pants and rain jacket, slip a cover over their backpack, and slosh along. The only catch is that most rain suits keep out air as well as water. Inside, you steam like a turkey roasting in a plastic bag.

Gore-Tex rain gear (see later in this chapter) does an admirable job of keeping you dry as long as you occasionally treat the seams with a sealer.

Cold-weather Wear

Cold-weather garments are designed chiefly to provide warmth. They may also protect against wind and wet, but their prime function is to retain body heat. In a heavy rain an additional water-repellent outer garment is usually required. Cold-weather wear uses many types of insulating materials (called fill or fillers), among them several kinds of down, synthetics, and other fluffy, air-trapping substances.

Down is a soft fuzz that grows close to the skin of duck, geese, and other waterfowl. Because of its superior insulating properties, its light weight, compressibility, and long life, down is a favored filler for outdooring wear and sleeping bags. Down's most serious shortcoming is a tendency to mat and lose its insulating qualities when wet. Therefore, it is imperative that down garments be kept dry. Wet, they are worthless for insulation.

Garments of 100 percent down are the warmest and the highest quality. They are also more costly than garments containing mixtures of down and feathers. A cautionary note: Make sure you get what you pay for.

Polyester is a synthetic fiber processed to give it loft: that is, to stay fluffy and trap dead air. For the same degree of insulation as down, polyester bulks more and weighs more. Furthermore, it is not as compressible as down and doesn't last as long. However, when wet, polyester filler does not mat or clump up. You can squeeze the water out of a polyester-filled garment and still be reasonably warm in it.

A jacket is, in effect, a mountain parka containing a filler; thus it gives warmth plus wind protection. A down or polyester "sweater" is similar to a jacket, only lighter and waist length. A "shirt" is lighter than a sweater; it has

The main function of cold-weather wear is the retention of body heat. The most efficient insulators are wool, down, and certain synthetic fibers.

shirtlike tails and can be worn as a jacket on slightly cool days. A "pullover"
is shorter than a shirt and has no full-length front opening; it is sometimes worn
as an undershirt on really cold days. A "vest" is a kind of fitted sleeveless shirt.
Lightest of the cold-weather garments, it is often worn under a mountain parka.

The variety of filled garments is mind-boggling to even experienced backpackers, especially when you add pants for extremely cold weather, mittens,
booties, and hoods. Decked out from head to toe in down- or polyester-filled
garments, you'd look like a balloon in Macy's parade. You'd also perish from
the heat unless you were atop Mount McKinley. Purchase and wear with
practicality in mind.

To cover your hands you can chose between mittens or gloves. Because
mittens prevent cold air from circulating between the fingers, they are warmer.
Gloves are useful when manual dexterity is needed, as when operating a camera.

Gaiters are a kind of zip-on ankle cuff. Short gaiters shield just your boot
tops and ankles; the long variety reaches from boot top to just below your knee.
Shorties are often worn when traveling over loose ground or across packed
snow. They help keep debris out of shoes. Longies are worn in deep, loose snow.
Overboots are stiff fabric shells that cover the calf and entire boot. They insulate
even better than gaiters and are worn in very deep snow and extremely cold
weather.

Like rainwear, gaiters and overboots do a good job of keeping snow and
water out, even though underneath them you may become wet with perspiration.

Headwear

"To keep your feet warm, wear a hat." It's a venerable saying, worn with age
but not worn out. I used to assume it was only an old hiker's tale until one cold
Canadian morning I slipped a stocking cap on my head and pulled it down
firmly. Within minutes my whole body was so warm I had to take off a wool
shirt.

I was surprised, though I shouldn't have been. At least a third of your body
heat loss is radiated from the head, even if you have plenty of hair. Cover your
head and conserve your heat.

One of the most useful cold-weather head covers is the wool stocking cap
or navy-type watch cap. If your ears and forehead get cold—as they will when
winter winds howl—pull the hat low. A stocking cap is also handy for night
wear when you want to keep your head out of the sleeping bag to watch the
stars. A balaclava is like a watch cap, only it has openings for eyes and mouth.

Pulled down, it gives you a Halloween look, but it will protect your face in a stinging, snowy wind.

For fair weather choose a "crusher" type of hat, or a tennis hat, something with a wide brim to shade forehead and eyes. A handkerchief hat made by knotting a bandanna at the corners will do a good job of shielding your head from the sun, and another bandanna rolled and tied around your forehead will absorb perspiration.

Miscellaneous Wear

To keep your pants from drooping you can wear a belt or suspenders (both, if you want to be doubly sure). Suspenders give a free feeling to your middle, but your pack may grind waist clips or buttons into your back.

If even in the wilderness you're too modest to skinny-dip, cram a light-weight swimsuit in the bottom of your pack. Or you can simply wear underwear.

Being larger than handkerchiefs, bandannas are much more versatile. In addition to being usable for head coverings or sweat bands, they come in handy as face towels, dish towels, hot-pot holders, emergency bandages, and water filters (to get the big chunks out, not the microscopic critters).

Cotton shoelaces last just so long, then begin fraying, and finally break at

The uses to which a bandanna can be put are virtually unlimited. Some of its more common applications: forehead sweat band, neck sun protection, handkerchief (tie one end to your belt rather than stuffing the whole thing into a pocket), utensil towel, water filter.

an inopportune time. Rather than knotting the break, carry a spare set of braided nylon laces, which seem to last forever.

Choosing Clothing

Seldom does a person suddenly decide, "I'm going to go backpacking!" and go to a mountaineering store to deck the body from head to toe. Like other backpacking gear, clothing is acquired piece by piece, some old, some new, some borrowed. Often it's a process of trial and error over months and years. For example, you acquire a flannel shirt at a rummage sale. Good fit, good price. But after a couple of trips you decide the shirt is just too thin, so you give it away. Or maybe you put up with it until it falls apart. Then you find another shirt, this one sturdier, warmer.

All clothing purchases should be dictated primarily by your needs. For example, if most of your backpacking is in temperate climates, do you really need that down jacket, or would a thin wool shirt suffice? Acquire—and carry —what you need, but use what you acquire. If, over a period, you don't use something, you probably don't need it.

When buying outdooring clothing, make sure you get a good fit. By "good" I mean comfortable. Not too loose, not too snug. Clothing that is too tight may chafe, bind, or cut off blood circulation. Too loose, and it'll be constantly snagging brush or tripping you. Never mind what sizes you normally wear in street shoes, dress shirts, or sport pants. In outdooring clothing, wear sizes that feel right on your body. On long treks your functional wardrobe is going to get a lot of use, so make sure it's going to stay comfortable.

Following are some details to look for in outdooring apparel.

Fabrics

Get the sturdiest, best-insulating, lightest-weight fabrics for the job you expect the garment to perform. Generally speaking, nylon is lightweight and strong but is a poor insulator. When wet it can be icy cold. Nylon-cotton blends are durable, and they dry fast, but they are only fair insulators.

If all your outdooring will be done in warm bone-dry weather, and if you seldom perspire, then under- and outerwear can be cotton. Dry cotton is soft to the touch, and, having loose fibers, it allows skin to breathe while being a fair insulator. But when cotton is wet—from rain or perspiration—it loses its insulating power and even conducts heat away from your body. In wet, cold weather, all-cotton clothing is bad news.

Wool may not be comfortable to your skin, and it is bulky. But wool has the curious characteristic of retaining body heat when wet. Wool contains water-repellent oils, and it is practically indestructible. For any cold-weather trips—even for multi-day hikes where there's a remote chance of rain—wool or wool-blend clothing is a must. Clothing that's 100 percent wool can be too hot and too heavy, so consider wool-and-synthetic blends that insulate well, dry quickly, and pack down into a tight space.

Gore-Tex is the trade name for a special material made by combining layers of fabric with a thin polymer film. Tiny pores in the polymer let molecules of water vapor—such as that given off by your body—pass out but prevent liquid water and wind from coming in. Outerwear, sleeping bag covers, and tents are often made from Gore-Tex.

Polyester fabrics are used for parkas, pants, pullovers, jackets, even hats. Polyesters are lightweight and soft, with a high warmth-to-weight ratio, and because they absorb very little water, they dry quickly.

Closures

Two types of zippers are commonly used on outdooring clothing. Coil zippers are smooth-operating, not susceptible to jamming, and continue to work in extremely cold weather. Ladder-tooth zippers are stronger, but metal ones may freeze up in cold weather. Look for garments with zippers that open or close from both top and bottom. Such closures provide good ventilation and access to inside pockets.

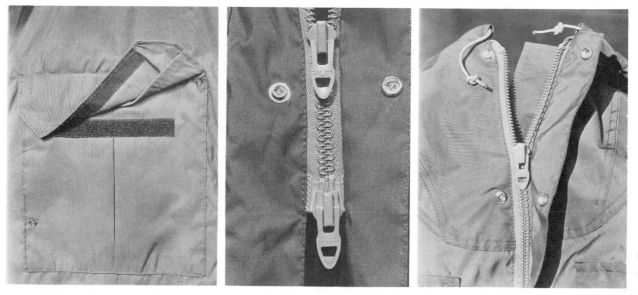

When choosing outerwear, pay attention to detailing. Fold-over pockets with hook-and-pile fastenings stay shut under almost any conditions; double zipper closures allow garments to be opened from either top or bottom (metal snaps give extra protection); double stitching adds more seam strength (and drawstrings hold clothing snugly against your body).

Snaps make strong closures, but be sure to check the fabric around them. It should be reinforced so it won't tear when a snap is popped open. Beware of snaps in plastic items, such as inexpensive ponchos. Most plastic won't take the strain involved in pulling snaps apart. Closures (such as jacket fronts) that have snaps as well as zippers give good protection against cold drafts.

Buttons are fine on shirts but not on outerwear or winterwear. Difficult to operate with cold-numbed fingers, buttons also have a perverse tendency to come off at the wrong time.

Hook-and-pile fastenings (called Velcro) are common on pockets and sleeve closures. Fairly secure, they are easy to open and close with mittened or cold hands.

Drawstrings are used in hoods, in parka waists, and in pullover bottoms. To secure them you can tie a knot or snug up a plastic cord lock.

Pockets

Pockets are for carrying smallish objects that you need to use frequently—things such as a notebook, pencil, knife, compass, insect repellent, sun cream. Pockets should therefore be roomy, easy to get into, and close at hand. Stylish though they may be, skintight slit openings and pants with no pockets at all are a pain, literally as well as figuratively, when you're fumbling for a handkerchief in freezing temperatures. Some outdooring pants have patch pockets with button-down flaps. These are very useful for carrying little items you have to grab as you walk along.

Jackets and parkas often have several kinds of storage compartments: cargo pockets for carrying large items, capacious back pockets for an extra shirt or lunch, vertical pockets for maps, insulated pockets for hand-warming. Except on the slip-in type of warming pocket, look for generous fold-over flaps and good closures (zippers, snaps, or Velcro), to keep snow out and personal objects in.

Seams and Stitching

Look for flat-fell seams, in which the fabric edges are folded around one another before being sewn down. Flat-fell seams actually have four layers of material through which the stitching passes (usually in two parallel rows), which gives them greater strength. This type of double stitching is most frequently seen on jeans. Seams should be sewn flat—that is, no gaps, no puckering, no raw edges.

Stitching should be straight and evenly spaced with no loose loops or raveled thread ends. (Even on a new garment an occasional thread end is inevitable, but cut it off rather than pull it or the whole seam may come undone.) Be sure to check stitching along zippers and around other fastenings, where strain is greatest. Extra stitching at zipper ends and pocket corners is a sign of good workmanship.

Several manufacturers put out do-it-yourself kits for making outdoor clothes (as well as sleeping bags and tents). Such kits contain everything necessary to assemble a garment, plus detailed instructions to guide your nimble, or not-so-nimble, fingers. In making a kit you not only enjoy the pleasure of seeing something come together in front of your very eyes, but you save as much as a third of the price of a comparable store-bought item.

A Lesson in Layering

Along with dehydrated foods, one of the greatest boons to outdooring is the clothing layering principle. It's a system of insulating your body to retain body heat by trapping layers of air between relatively thin articles of clothing. When you feel too cold, you add layers; when you feel too warm, you subtract layers. This putting on and taking off is a continuous operation that goes on all day as you warm up or cool down.

Fine-tune your comfort by adding or subtracting layers of lightweight clothing as the weather and your level of activity change. The first layer, next to your skin, should trap dead air for warmth close to the body. Long johns are a good choice for an inner clothing layer. Articles in the second layer should be wool or fluffy polyester, and might comprise a lightweight shirt worn with trousers or knickers, a hat, and mittens. A third layer provides additional insulation during rest periods and extreme cold; a parka or vest with down or synthetic filling "breathes" well yet gives good insulation. The fourth layer—the outer shell of your system—should keep out wind and water. Mountain parkas or Gore-Tex garments are excellent windbreakers. (Adapted from material provided by Woolrich, Inc.)

Keeping your body at a comfortable temperature by donning or doffing layers of lightweight clothing may sound strange, but it works.

An example: Rising in the morning before the sun has smiled on your campsite, you slip a long-sleeved cotton shirt over your T-shirt and add a sweater. In an hour or so you warm up sufficiently to peel off the sweater. By noon the sun is nearly overhead, so you get rid of the long-sleeved shirt. Sitting around camp in the evening you feel a bit cool, so on goes the shirt, and perhaps the sweater. If a breeze picks up, you add a windbreaker.

Adding or subtracting clothing layers
is a quick-change technique
easily performed on or off the trail.

The same applies to your lower body. Chilly with one pair of pants? Put on your second pair as well. And if temperatures really drop, long underwear plus pants will make you super cozy.

Such fiddling around with clothing throughout the day may seem like a hassle, but after a little while it becomes second nature. Around camp it's no trouble hopping in or out of clothes, and on the trail you develop your own quick-change techniques. Stop, put down pack, take off sweater and stuff it under a pack strap (don't put it inside if you think you'll need it later), don pack, and you're on your way.

Since backpacking is a matter of conserving weight, choose clothes with versatility in mind, making every garment serve as many purposes as possible. Think not just of an item's own function but also how it can be layered with other garments.

Walking and Carrying

In the woods you meet up with walkers of all persuasions and paces. Some idle along the trail, in no great hurry to get anywhere. Others thunder through the bush, hell-bent on reaching distant peaks and returning in record time. After a break-in of only a trip or two, you will settle into a natural style of walking befitting your own body and soul. You don't need instruction in that. It'll be what feels right to you. Still, a few tips on walking may ease that break-in period.

A WORD ABOUT WALKING

The art of pack carrying begs for halfway decent posture so you can keep going without undue fatigue and muscle strain. Apart from repose—the most relaxing position of all—the human body is at its greatest ease in a vertical attitude. Especially when walking.

With head up, your shoulders should be relaxed, dropped back, rather than hunched up. Arms should dangle in a natural, loose kind of way. If they happen to swing of their own accord, let them. But don't make a conscious effort to force them into an exaggerated swing or you may

Carrying a full load on an extended hike isn't as difficult as it may appear, providing you use a well-fitted pack, loaded properly.

throw yourself into some weird, unbalanced gait. Keep your body straight, and, as Mother would say, don't slouch.

Legs? Again, avoid forcing them into any kind of stride. Just let them swing from the hips rather than kicking out from the knees.

Adjust your backpack and clothing until they settle into the right place and you can forget about them. Take strides that suit your legs and the terrain, moving at a pace that feels right to you. In less than a mile you'll establish a walking rhythm that blends pace, stride, and breathing and shifts its inner gears with changes in the land.

Speed? That depends on how far away your goal is and how much time you've allowed yourself to get there. In your pre-trip planning you will of course have figured how far you want to travel in a day without pushing yourself, allowing for ups and downs in elevation that will decrease or increase your trail time. As a very rough guide, figure on two miles per hour when slogging along steadily on a level trail.

Learn to visually take in and enjoy everything around you while still keeping one eye on where you're going. Hikers have become so enthralled with a view that they've wandered beyond a turn in the trail. Very embarrassing, especially when the trail is on a steep slope.

Plant your feet firmly. A log or rock in your path? Step over rather than on the object, in case it's wobbly.

If the going gets steep, take shorter steps and lean forward from the waist to keep the pack weight over your feet. When the grade really increases and you start puffing, use the rest step. Step forward, lean your weight over that foot while straightening the leg, rest for a second, bring the other foot forward, lean over it, straighten the leg, rest, and so on.

At altitudes of 5,000 feet or greater, concentrate on breathing regularly

Interested in knowing just how far you walk? Wear a pedometer on your belt and adjust it for your own stride.

Your enjoyment of the outdoors depends greatly on how much you relax while walking. Hold your head up, keep your back straight, and let your legs swing easily from the hips.

and deeply. Without plenty of air in your system, you may develop a nagging headache.

Hiking downhill is usually easier than uphill trekking, and your pace will pick up considerably. But be wary of tippy rocks, large and small. Also, pounding downhill on your heels for a long while may jar your spine until you develop a headache, so even though you're eager to reach camp, take it easy. On loose debris or on snow you can sometimes manage a controlled slide on your feet. Just make sure you're well balanced and that you can stop without coming in sudden contact with a boulder.

Cross-country travel, also known as bushwhacking, can be rougher than trail hiking. The ground under your feet may have lumps, holes, or both; it may be slippery. You may have to push your way through brush, wade a stream, or scramble up a steep bank, using hands as well as feet. Rugged as it may seem, bushwhacking has its own set of joys, not the least of which is traveling over territory that not everyone treads.

RESTING AND SNACKING

Whether hiking on or off trail, don't run yourself ragged. After all, backpacking is supposed to be a pleasurable affair with nature, not a grueling forced march. If you feel tired, pause and take a breather. For a jiffy rest, lean your pack on a rock or against a tree and catch your breath for a couple of minutes. If you're really getting punchy from a steep slog, remove your pack. Stretch your arms and shoulders to unkink tight muscles. Sit down until your breathing returns to normal and your heart stops pounding. But don't flop for longer than about ten minutes or you'll have one helluva time making yourself move again.

Regarding lunching and munching during a trek, there are several theories. One is the steam-locomotive theory that advocates shoveling in fuel continuously to keep the fire stoked. That is, as you move along you nibble, munch, snack, never pausing for a midday meal but constantly stowing away the goodies while you walk. The other is the factory-lunch-break theory, whose subscribers call a halt around noon, or whenever hunger pangs become fierce. If you're such a hiker, you set down your pack, find a comfortable seat, loosen your boots, ceremoniously break out the salami, cheese, sardines, and crackers, and make an event out of dining. Perhaps the most effective system combines the two. Do eat, for if you don't provide your body with energy, it'll falter and balk.

After eating lunch, rest for half an hour to allow food to settle in your stomach. But not much longer, or your body will try to convince you it's had enough walking for one day.

One of the keys to pleasant hiking is the brief rest stop. Take five minutes or so, just enough time for a short breather and a long drink.

And be sure to drink plenty of liquids while trekking. You might not feel you're perspiring mightily, but with every exhalation your body loses water. Below 85 degrees F (30 degrees C), you're not likely to fall ill from dehydration. Still, be kind to yourself. Swig often from your water bottle, whatever the temperature.

THE FIRST DAY OUT

For most people, being in the backcountry means adapting to different waking hours and bedding-down hours, to different kinds of physical activity, to different climatic situations. Such unfamiliar conditions take some time getting used to, so be prepared for your body to react accordingly.

A hiking staff is a handy aid for walking downhill, uphill, or on the flat. It gives added balance and acts as a "third leg."

For example, the first day out may seem—to put it mildly—difficult. Your pack weighs you down. Aches and pains not only develop, they persist. You become tired early in the day. You grow grouchy.

Don't despair! It's only that your body requires a period of acclimation. It needs to get used to a new regime. One way to help your system over the first-day blahs is to forget back-home eating habits and provide your body with carbohydrates throughout the day. In addition to breakfast, lunch, and dinner, you should continuously nibble, snack, and munch to replenish burned-off energy.

Most athletes are familiar with a dietary technique whereby the body can be supercharged to handle a period of intense physical activity. Called carbohydrate loading, it has to do with first lowering the body's glycogen, or animal starch level, and then supplying the body with an overabundance of glycogen.

About a week before the start of a trip, dedicate a day to fairly strenuous exercise. Without wearing yourself to a frazzle, play some tennis, jog, swim some laps, bike, or take a long hike. For the next two or three days avoid eating starches and sugars. Then, on the final three or four days, load up on carbohydrates by consuming plenty of breads, pastry, pasta, cereals, potatoes, and rice. This will raise your body's glycogen level significantly, providing the extra fuel to tide you over that first day.

WALKING AIDS

I've noticed that most backpackers seem to prefer walking empty-handed. Once in a while, though, I've met with hikers carrying a staff or long stick. "Gives extra support," they say. "Acts as a kind of third leg for better balance."

A handy length for a hiking staff is shoulder-high to head-high. Anything longer can be unwieldy, and anything shorter isn't of great use. Inch-diameter bamboo makes a stout, lightweight staff, but any sturdy bit of tree branch will do if it's reasonably straight.

Walking across steep snowfields or on glaciers sometimes calls for an ice ax, which is used not so much as a staff as for a brake in case of a fall. Ice axes, crampons, snowshoes, and skis are specialized pieces of winter mountaineering gear whose use is beyond the scope of this book. If in your backpacking you have to cross a snow slope, kicking steps will usually suffice. As you punch your boots firmly into the snow, keep the soles flat and parallel with the earth's surface, not with the slope, to minimize slippage. That means standing up straight, keeping body weight directly over your feet, instead of leaning into the mountainside.

When walking on snowy slopes kick your boots in, keeping the soles parallel with the earth's surface; when wearing crampons, keep boot soles parallel with the slope.

A belt pack, worn either in front or in back, is handy for carrying such small items as a camera, notebook, lunch, and the first-aid kit. A day pack is used for short hikes close to home or out of base camp. Day packs are also handy for youngsters willing to tote their share of a family load.

ABOUT BACKPACKS

Human hands are marvelous devices for gripping, but as anyone who has wrestled a heavy suitcase through an airport knows, hands weren't designed to lug bulky loads very far. Perhaps hips and shoulders weren't either, but they are better burden bearers than hands.

Though "backpack" seems to be the best word for our burden carrying, it is a bit misleading. A horse can take considerable weight directly on its back, but not a human. That's why full-sized outdooring packs are made so that their weight is mostly divided between hips and shoulders, with only a small part of it going to the back.

A bewildering array of pack sizes, shapes, and types awaits the innocent who first wanders into a well-equipped outdooring shop. A brief guided tour, progressing from small to large, may help put things in perspective.

Belt Packs

Not really a backpack, a belt pack is a pouch affair that fastens around your waist. Just roomy enough to hold lunch, a first-aid kit, and a few other small items, a belt pack is handy for short strolls. Skiers like them because they are compact and easy to get into. Worn with the pouch in back, a belt pack is termed a fanny pack; in front, a belly pack.

Day Packs

A day pack is a lightweight sack with shoulder straps (which should be adjustable), small enough to be fitted into a larger backpack yet roomy enough to hold lunch, a water bottle, a sweater, an essentials kit, and a camera. Some day packs have zippered compartments and pockets; others are more like bags with a drawstring closure. Because a day pack puts most of the weight on the shoulders, it isn't intended for heavy, bulky loads. Though not necessary, a stabilizing strap that fastens around the waist will keep the pack from shifting with body movement.

Rucksacks

Used more in Europe than in the United States, a rucksack is an uncompartmented pack, roomy enough to hold several days' worth of gear. All its weight hangs from your shoulders, much of it pressing into your spine. Also, unless the back of a rucksack is padded and it is packed carefully, cook pots and containers may gouge your kidneys. Despite such shortcomings, many oldtimers wouldn't use anything but a rucksack.

A frame rucksack has stiff supports (sometimes internal, sometimes external) that give the pack some structure and help keep it away from your back. Still, since dead weight hangs mostly from the shoulders, rucksack wearers tend to lean forward as they walk in order to keep the center of gravity over their feet. Even without a pack, a confirmed rucksacker appears to be looking for something on the ground.

A soft pack, such as that on the right, molds itself to the contours of your back, keeping the load weight close to your center of gravity.

Soft Packs

Sturdily made for lugging considerable gear, soft packs have no visible support but usually contain padding to protect your tender back and internal stays, rods, or shells for rigidity. Some designs depend on a tightly packed load for support. Some have one large compartment into which you jam almost everything—clothing, cooking gear, food, and such—lashing sleeping bag and shelter outside. This kind of packing calls for practice, patience, and skill because inevitably the item you want will be at the very bottom. Two- or three-compartment soft packs offer a little more control over what's stuffed in them.

Because they're designed for moderately heavy loads, soft packs have a sturdy hip belt that allows much of the weight to be taken off your shoulders. With a little practice you can learn to change the weight distribution by adjusting hip and shoulder straps as you walk. On level ground, keep both sets of straps snugged up for equal weight distribution. If the grade steepens, loosen the hip belt and lean into the load with your shoulders. Going downhill, loosen the shoulder straps and cinch up the waist strap to take most of the weight on your hips.

If your spine gets hot from the pack's resting flat against it, loosening the shoulder straps will let the load hinge at your hips, thus allowing air to circulate between it and your back.

When properly stuffed, soft packs are quite comfortable because they conform to the contours of the upper body, moving as it moves. Soft packs are preferred by many climbers, cross-country snowshoers, skiers, and cross-country backpackers who like a flexible, snug, back-hugging load. I use a soft pack for short trips over rugged terrain, a frame pack for long treks or extended trail hikes.

Shoulder-strap attachments on soft packs will sometimes give way under extra-heavy loads. Once, after cramming my soft pack with some weighty stuff, I picked it up by the shoulder straps, only to have straps and pack part company. Luckily I was at home and not in the backcountry, so I transferred everything to my frame pack.

To find out if you'd be happy with a soft pack, rent or borrow one, load it up, and take a weekend hike. Soft packs are made in different sizes, so be sure to get a proper fit or you'll feel like a turtle looks.

External Frame Packs

The typical external frame pack has two parts: an external frame made of aluminum or magnesium tubing, molded plastic, or wood, and a pack bag. The pack bag holds whatever gear you want to load it with. The frame gives shape and support to the pack bag, transferring its loaded weight to your body. A few packs feature external/internal frames or so-called convertible frames, but the nomenclature of such hybrids is as complex as their configuration. Most of the following discussion applies to the regular external frame pack, the most widely used outdooring design.

The Frame

The most popular type of backpack frame is a rectangular ladderlike affair made of welded metal. One side of it attaches to the pack bag; the other side attaches—by means of shoulder straps and hip belt—to you. There are at least four types of external frames: the straight ladder, the contoured-S frame, the hip wrap (also called the wraparound), and the figure eight.

Most simple of all, the straight ladder frame consists of two straight, vertical side members and three horizontal members. Found on most lower-priced packs, the straight ladder frame does the basic job of transferring a pack's loaded weight to your hips and shoulders.

However, since no one's spine is ramrod straight, pack designers developed

EXTENSION BAR

SMOOTH WELDED JOINT

CLEVIS PIN PACK BAG CONNECTOR

PADDED SHOULDER STRAP

MESH BACK BOUND

PADDED HIP BELT

QUICK RELEASE BUCKLE

The external frame pack is perhaps the most versatile load carrier for long treks. The pack bag and its pockets hold everything you'll need; the frame gives support to the pack bag and transfers its weight to your hips.

STORM FLAP

WEATHER FLAP OVER ZIPPERED POCKET

WEATHER FLAP OVER COMPARTMENT ZIPPER

BACK POCKET

CRAMPON LASH PATCH

ICE AXE LOOP

a contoured-S frame, whose vertical members are curved somewhat the way your spine curves. Result: a better fit and a better weight distribution.

The hip-wrap frame is a contoured-S frame whose vertical members curve smoothly inward at the bottom to extend around your hips. The hip belt attaches farther forward than on other types, and this supposedly transfers more load weight to the hips. One catch is that if you have narrow hips, or are exceedingly broad in the beam, this type of frame may not fit properly. Another catch is that if you should take a sideways fall (not an uncommon occurrence even among trail veterans), the wraparound sections could give you a nasty bruise.

When set down on reasonably level ground, a pack with a hip-wrap frame will stand up by itself, a feature attractive to hikers who don't like to bend way down in doffing and donning their burden.

The figure-eight frame has sides that curve in toward each other, then out again, in hourglass fashion. At the narrowest part is attached a molded plastic swivel joint designed to even out movement between the pack and your hips. How well this system works to ease your load is up to you. Some backpackers can't detect any comfort differential between the figure-eight frame and the contoured-S frame. Some backpackers claim the former is the greatest advance since shoes. Try both and decide for yourself.

Attached to just about any decent external frame—and designed principally to distribute the load's weight—is a three-part suspension system consisting of the following:

1. A pair of padded, adjustable shoulder straps that puts some of the weight on your shoulders and helps keep the top of the pack from lurching as *you* lurch.

2. A hip belt (some are padded, some not) that carries most of the weight and holds the lower part of the pack snugly against the lower part of your body. Hip belts can be one-, two-, or three-piece and have different styles of buckles. All are pretty much equal in what they do, so choose the kind that suits you.

3. Single or double backbands stretched horizontally across the frame's vertical side members that ease a small part of the weight against your back and hold the frame away from your body. You have a choice of padded bands, mesh bands, or fabric bands.

On most frames, the shoulder straps, hip belts, and backbands are removable, so if you don't like one kind you can try another.

A few frames have straps that connect from the two shoulder straps across the chest. The idea is to help stabilize the load, but snugged across my sternum, chest straps restrict my breathing and give me claustrophobia of the wishbone.

The Pack Bag

The pack bag is the boxlike fabric container that comes in flashy colors, and has all those zippers and pockets, and hangs on the front of the pack frame. The pack bag is what holds your gear. Pack bags load from the top (handy when the pack is standing) or from the front (you usually lay them flat for loading or unloading). Top loaders may have one deep compartment or two shallower ones, each with its own zipper. The latter style allows you to better organize the contents; for example, clothing can go in one chamber, cooking gear in the other. A front loader may have a horizontal zipper or a horseshoe-shaped one that allows you to open the compartment like a suitcase and see where everything is without fumbling into corners.

Most pack bags have external pockets sewn right to them. These are the backpacker's helpmates, for they hold all those little items that are easily buried in a main compartment or are needed often. In the pockets you'd probably stow your water bottle, toilet paper, trail snacks, and such. A few pack bags have flat inside pockets for things you don't need to grab quickly.

The section of extra fabric at the top of a pack bag is called a storm flap. It protects the contents of the upper compartment even when the contents bulge out. Storm flaps are cinched down with straps or drawstrings.

Sewn to the outside of a pack bag may be several nifty-looking, slotted leather patches. These are "lash points," designed for carrying extra gear such as shelter stakes, a ground cloth, fishing rods, crampons. You fasten the items on by running straps or cords through the slots. A fabric loop near the bottom of the bag is for securing an ice ax.

The most widely used method of attaching pack bag to frame is that of fitting clevis pins (they look like thick cut-off nails with a hole in one end) through holes and locking them with a wire or split ring. This may look like a hokey arrangement, but it works very well, allowing the pack bag to be removed for repair or whatever. Carrying a few spare clevis pins and rings is a good idea.

Some pack bags are equipped with compression straps which can be adjusted to cinch the load and take strain off zippers.

Accessories and Extras

Top-quality packs will repel moisture, but no pack—no matter how well made—is entirely waterproof. In a steady downpour, water will eventually find a way in: through seams, through zippers, even through weather flaps. Sodden clothing or a soaked sleeping bag may sound humorous, but it can be disastrous.

You can cover yourself and your pack with a poncho, but ponchos flap in a stiff wind. The surest way to keep water out of your pack is to protect it with a rain cover. For big packs you can buy a ready-made rain cover, complete with drawstrings and snaps, or if you're handy with a sewing machine, you can make your own from treated nylon.

An umbrella in the wild may seem odd, but experienced trekkers in Nepal, New Zealand, and Australia have found an umbrella to be ideal protection against rain as well as against sun. Don't use an umbrella in a lightning storm. In such storms, lay low until the worst weather is over.

Elastic shock cords are also handy for fastening bulky gear to your backpack. Wrap them around the object and hook them to the pack frame or a lash point. But make sure they are snug, or things will bounce as you walk. Sturdy plastic bags and stuff sacks (fabric bags with drawstrings) are some of backpacking's most useful items, and you should own several in varied sizes. To keep things reasonably organized in your pack, stow essentials, toilet and repair articles, kitchen gear, consumables, sleeping bag, shelter, and shelter stakes in different-colored stuff sacks. It'll help avoid Easter egg hunts when you need to find something.

Picking a Pack

The time has come for you to make the plunge and buy a full-fledged backpack. A good pack will last a long time, so take your time in deciding which one you want to put your money in.

What are your backpacking aims and your gear-carrying needs? In other words, what kind of hiking do you expect to do? If most of your travels will be on trails, an external frame pack is perhaps best, whereas if you prefer rugged bushwhacking, consider the more stable soft pack.

Short trips don't call for big packs, so beware of overbuying. If you do, you'll either be carrying empty space or filling that space needlessly to justify it. A rough guide is 3,000 to 4,000 cubic inches of pack-bag volume for extended trips of a week or longer. For trips of two to three days, 2,000 to 3,000 cubic inches will suffice.

Take plenty of time to shop around, inspecting different styles, different models. Try packs on, loading them with the small sandbags available for that purpose. You should be able to put on and take off a loaded pack without a struggle. Practice will improve your technique, but even in the store if you experience real difficulties maneuvering a pack up and down, it may not be the

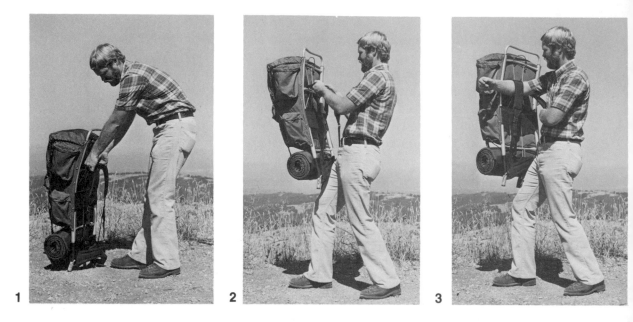

1   2   3

right one for you. Remember that packs and frames come in sizes, so be sure to get the one that fits your body. Weigh the opinions of experienced backpackers and salespeople, but settle on the pack that *feels* right. Of course, the ultimate test is on the trail. Though you can't field-test and return new equipment, you can rent packs. Each outdooring shop prefers a particular brand, so go to different stores.

External frames should have no sharp bends that, when continuously flexed, might fatigue and break. Welded joints should be strong and smooth so they won't snag the pack bag or your clothing. The suspension system should feel comfortable when the pack is weighted down. Shoulder straps should have spongy padding at least 2 inches wide and ¾ inch thick.

Check a pack bag's durability. The fabric should be sturdy but not overly heavy. Tightly woven nylon is lightweight and durable. Cordura—a coarser nylon—is sturdier. Cotton is heavier than nylon but less resistant to wear. Canvas is rugged but heavy. Look inside the pack bag for a shiny surface. This means the fabric is "waterproof," but to keep really hard rains out you should use a pack cover. Sewn seams should be tight and straight. Zipper ends and pocket corners should be reinforced. Zippers, whether metal or plastic, should operate smoothly.

Look for accessories and options that may be useful on long treks or expedition-type trips: lash points, ice ax loops, extra pockets, ski slots, an extension bar for tying on extra gear.

4

Donning a pack is a four-part operation carried out in one smooth motion. First, grasp the shoulder straps to lift the pack. Second, lift the pack to a rest position on one knee. Third, slip your arm under the shoulder strap. Fourth, slide the pack over your other arm and let it settle into place on your shoulders.

Loading a Pack

Each time you load equipment you'll find more efficient ways to stow things. A general rule is: last in, first out. That is, stow items you need first in the pack last, or stow them in the side pockets. A sleeping bag usually goes in the lowest compartment or is fastened below the pack bag. Lash sleeping pad and shelter on top. For trail hiking, try to pack heavy gear low for more stability.

Pack care is straightforward. Keep your pack away from fire, stand it up when you're not wearing it, and cover it in a heavy rain. You can wash a pack bag with detergent and warm water, but rinse it thoroughly; then, while the bag is still wet, fit it on the frame to dry.

CARING FOR CARRYING MUSCLES

During the first couple of days of a heavy trek your leg muscles may stiffen. Walking out the tightness is the best cure for that. Another backpacker's malady is sore shoulders, and time usually takes care of them; they become used to being loaded.

An aching back is more fretful because, when especially painful, it can keep you tossing and groaning at night when you should be sleeping. Almost

1   2   3

always an aching back is caused by an improperly loaded or badly adjusted pack.

On a loaded frame pack, shoulder straps should angle upward slightly from shoulder to frame, not pull down. The waist strap should circle you at your belt line and place most of the pack's weight on your hips. As you hike, occasionally hunch your shoulders and, while sucking your belly in, push out with the small of your back. Also, as you walk, occasionally shift the pack's weight from your shoulders to your hips by tightening the hip belt and loosening the shoulder straps. After a while, shift some of the weight back to your shoulders. It sounds simple, but you'll be surprised at how much your back will appreciate this.

Of course, if your back really bugs you, call a halt, perhaps for the rest of the day.

As you hike along, occasionally hook your thumbs in your shoulder straps to let the blood drain out of your hands.

4

Adjusting a frame pack, once it's on, requires that it be positioned properly. As shown in the front view at 1, the shoulder bar should be level with the top of your shoulders, the straps leading straight back. The side view, at 2, shows the correct shoulder-strap angle and waist-strap location. Hunch up your shoulders, as at 3, while connecting and tightening the waist straps. When your shoulders are relaxed, as at 4, the waist strap should rise at a slight angle from the side attachment.

Much outdooring pleasure derives from using map, compass, landmarks, and a great deal of common sense to find out where you are.

Navigating and Weathering

At one time or another, every backpacker experiences anxiety pangs about being out in the wild and getting lost. It's a natural emotion for humans conditioned to city streets and mechanized transportation. Being lost is mostly a matter of not knowing where you are. Therefore, it figures that as long as you know where you are, you're not lost. (*Thinking* you know where you are is another story, one we'll get into later in the chapter.) How can a backpacker know at any time where he or she is? Not by dropping bread crumbs or unraveling string, but by using common sense and a few navigational aids.

BACKCOUNTRY NAVIGATION

First, common sense. In the northern hemisphere the sun and the moon are, during fall, winter, and spring, generally south of you, rising in a southeasterly direction and setting in a southwesterly direction. During summer they rise in the *north*east and set in the *north*west. At any time of the year, sun and moon are due south at their high-

117

At any time of the year, in the northern hemisphere, the sun is generally south of you, a good common-sense indication of direction.

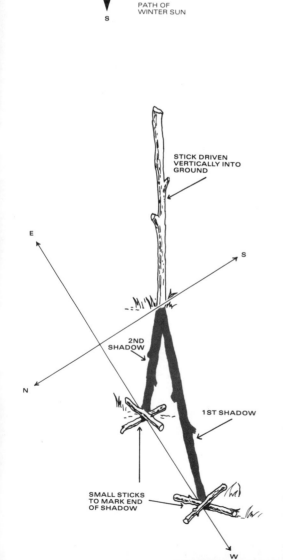

N

E

PATH OF
SUMMER SUN

W

SUN'S
HIGHEST POINT
IS AT NOON

PATH OF
WINTER SUN

S

To tell direction with a nondigital-readout watch, face the sun and point the hour hand toward it. In the direction you're facing, south lies halfway between the hour hand and twelve o'clock. If you're on daylight saving time, south is halfway between the hour hand and one o'clock.

SOUTH

SUN

NORTH

STICK DRIVEN
VERTICALLY INTO
GROUND

E

S

2ND
SHADOW

N

1ST SHADOW

SMALL STICKS
TO MARK END
OF SHADOW

W

A stick shadow can give you an accurate indication of direction. Push a stick vertically into the ground and mark where the tip of its shadow falls. After the shadow has moved several inches, mark its tip again. A line connecting the two marks will run east and west, east being in the direction of the second mark. Another line perpendicular to the first will run north and south.

est point. Thus, as long as either is visible you can tell direction in a vague sort
of way. This doesn't guarantee you won't ever get lost, but it's a bit of basic knowledge that should make you feel a little more secure in the wild.

Forget about looking for moss on the north side of trees. Moss can be found growing on any and all sides of a tree and therefore is seldom a reliable indicator of direction. Instead, in forested areas, look for slopes on which vegetation is richer or greener. That'll be the north side, because it receives fewer direct rays of the sun and so tends to be more lush, less dry.

You can use a nondigital-readout watch to tell general direction in the northern hemisphere. Holding the watch flat, face the sun and point the hour hand toward it. In the direction you're facing, halfway between the hour hand and twelve o'clock—if you're on standard time—is due south. If you're on daylight saving time, south is halfway between the hour hand and one o'clock.

Another fairly reliable method of telling direction in the northern hemisphere involves nothing more sophisticated than a straight stick and the sun. Of course, if the sun isn't shining, you'll just have to wait until it appears.

Push the stick vertically into the ground until it stands up by itself, then mark the tip of its shadow on the ground. After waiting twenty minutes or so, mark the shadow's tip again. Now connect the two points with a straight line, which will run east–west, east being in the direction of the second mark. Remember, the sun moves east to west, so shadows cast by it will move in the opposite direction.

The Orienteering Compass

Any compass will give you an indication of north, but for backcountry navigation you need more help than that. A compass suitable for wilderness navigation should have the following features:

1. A rotating housing with cardinal points (N, E, S, W) marked on the upper rim, and a degree dial marked on the lower rim, reading in a clockwise direction. (A compass reading in a counterclockwise direction is known as a forester's compass and should not be used for backpacking.)

2. Within the housing, a liquid-dampened needle with a colored north-seeking end.

3. On the bottom of the housing, an orienting arrow.

4. Beneath the housing, a transparent baseplate with a direction-of-travel arrow and with straight edges.

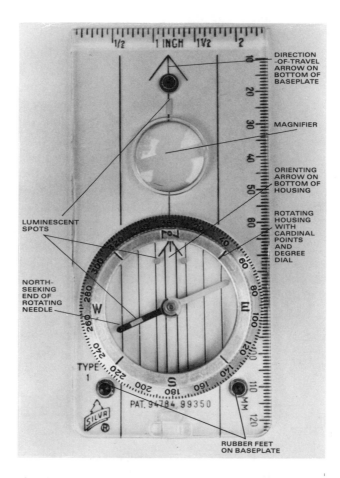

DIRECTION -OF-TRAVEL ARROW ON BOTTOM OF BASEPLATE

MAGNIFIER

ORIENTING ARROW ON BOTTOM OF HOUSING

ROTATING HOUSING WITH CARDINAL POINTS AND DEGREE DIAL

LUMINESCENT SPOTS

NORTH- SEEKING END OF ROTATING NEEDLE

TYPE 1

PAT. 94784 99350

RUBBER FEET ON BASEPLATE

A good wilderness navigation compass should have a rotating housing (bezel) marked with cardinal compass points and degrees, a liquid-dampened needle with a colored north-seeking end, an orienting arrow marked on the bottom of the rotating housing, and a transparent baseplate marked with a direction-of-travel arrow.

Because a compass contains a metal needle that tends to align itself with the earth's magnetic field, other metallic or magnetic objects may deflect the needle, resulting in erroneous readings. A nearby pocketknife, watch, belt buckle, zipper, camera, or camera light meter can cause errors, as can another compass. If your compass needle swings erratically, check for such objects.

Backcountry Navigation

A map, compass, or altimeter is of limited use by itself. But put these elements together and you'll have an unbeatable combination that can tell you where you are, where you've been, even where you want to go.

To orient a map (see page 122, top), that is, to turn it with its magnetic north lined up with the compass so the map's features are "oriented" the same as the surrounding countryside:

1. Open the topo and lay it out flat, away from metallic objects.

2. Rotate the compass degree dial until 360° (and N) aligns with the direction-of-travel arrow on the compass baseplate.

3. Place the compass on the map's declination diagram, with one side edge of the baseplate exactly against the magnetic north (MN) line, and with the direction-of-travel arrow pointing toward the top of the map.

4. Rotate the map and compass *together* until the compass north-seeking needle aligns with the direction-of-travel arrow (and N). The map is now oriented, and degree readings of features on the map are the same as those of the actual points on the compass.

Congratulations—you've just eliminated true north, and you won't have to think about it again.

Now find the elevation of your location on the map, and set your altimeter according to the printed contour line at that point.

Next, without moving the map, slide the compass to the map area you'll be hiking, keeping the north-seeking needle aligned with N.

Pencil a secondary magnetic north line along one edge of the compass baseplate, and mark its top "MN." You can use this new line to re-orient the

To orient your map and yourself, point the direction-of-travel arrow away from you and rotate the entire compass until that arrow and the north end of the needle line up. Keeping this alignment, lay the compass on the map, with one compass edge against the vertical line of the map's declination diagram. Now rotate map and compass together until the north-seeking end of the needle aligns with the direction-of-travel arrow (and N). (See text for step-by-step procedure.)

Triangulation pinpoints your location at the intersection of three lines representing bearings on identified landmarks (see text for step-by-step procedure). In the example shown, bearings taken on three prominent peaks intersect on a trail.

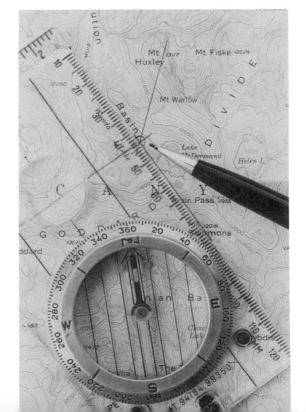

map in the field without unfolding it.

To take a map bearing to establish a direction of travel from point A (where you are) to point B (where you want to go):

1. Draw a light pencil line on the map from A to B, and place the compass on the map with one of its edges along this line.

2. Rotate the compass degree dial until the orienting arrow and the grid lines on the bottom of the housing are parallel to the secondary magnetic north line. (The tip of the orienting arrow should point toward the top of the map, not the bottom.)

3. Read the bearing on the degree dial at the direction-of-travel arrow.

To travel an established bearing to get from one place to another:

1. Set the established bearing on the compass degree dial at the direction-of-travel arrow.

2. Hold the compass flat in front of your body, with the direction-of-travel arrow pointing straight ahead.

3. Rotate your body and the compass together until the north-seeking needle and the tip of the orienting arrow are aligned.

4. Pick a prominent feature (such as a large tree), if the direction-of-travel arrow points to one, or have a companion walk ahead and stand as a marker. Whichever kind of feature you use, walk up to it.

5. Repeat steps 1 through 4, periodically checking your location by referring to your map and altimeter. In this manner, just leapfrog to your destination in a more or less straight line.

To take a compass bearing on a physical feature in order to establish a direction to it:

1. Hold the compass flat in front of your body, the direction-of-travel arrow pointed straight ahead.

2. Rotate your body and the compass together until the direction-of-travel arrow points to the chosen feature.

3. Rotate the degree dial until N aligns with the north-seeking needle.

4. Read the bearing on the degree dial at the direction-of-travel arrow.

To locate yourself on a map by triangulation (see page 122, bottom):

1. Look around the surrounding physical landscape and find three prominent permanent features (such as a lake, a peak, a pass) not close together and not on the same line of sight with you.

2. Locate the features on the map. The map may be oriented, but it does not have to be.

3. Take a compass bearing on one feature. Draw a line on the map through that feature on the same bearing. You are somewhere along that line.

4. Repeat steps 2 and 3 with the other features. Where the three lines intersect is where you are.

5. Check the map contour lines at the intersection point, then verify the reading with your altimeter.

Map and Compass Tips

Using map and compass properly is a highly satisfying outdooring skill. In fact, some people enjoy navigating so much, their chief reason for backpacking is to find their way over hill and dale. As you become proficient with the tools and confident of your ability to navigate, you'll develop your own techniques and shortcuts. Meanwhile, here are a few tips to streamline things.

1. If you expect to operate across more than one topographic map, trim off the map margins and fasten adjacent sheets together, edge to edge, with clear tape.

2. After plotting out your trip at home, fold the map or maps to a convenient size that allows any portion to be quickly available. To protect a map, slip it into a clear plastic bag.

3. Orient your map before hitting the trail.

4. Keep map, compass, and a pencil in a readily accessible place, where you can reach them without stopping to take off your pack.

5. At trailhead, where you know your position, identify prominent landmarks and orient the map.

6. As you hike, pause frequently to consult the map or compass and

To protect a topo map yet have it usable at all times, keep it folded inside a clear plastic bag.

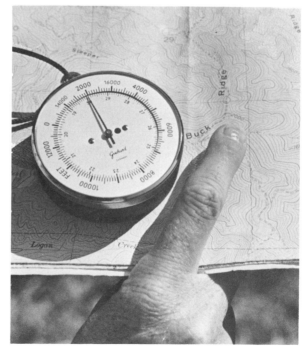

An altimeter shows elevation, giving you a three-dimensional wilderness location.

establish your whereabouts (every ten to fifteen minutes is usually adequate unless you need an exact location). But don't stumble along looking at them, lest you run off or into something.

7. Each time you fix your location, check the map for features yet to come so you'll recognize them. As you walk, watch for these features.

If you're interested in learning more about orienteering—either as a back-country skill or as an outdooring sport in itself—I suggest reading *Be Expert with Map and Compass* by Björn Kjellström (New York: Charles Scribner's Sons, 1976).

The Altimeter

Compass and map orient you in two dimensions. Locations on the earth's surface can also be measured in a third dimension—elevation. An altimeter gives you a reading of elevation, thus allowing you to pinpoint yourself in three dimensions.

Not many backpackers take the time to fiddle with map, compass, and altimeter, but those who do swear by the extra instrument. Operating on atmospheric pressure, an altimeter does have the drawback of being affected by changes in the weather, so remember that an impending storm can give a false reading of elevation.

If You Become Lost

"All this about landmarks and navigation and gadgets is well and good," you mutter. "But what happens if sometime I really don't know where I am? What if I do get lost?"

Unless you've fallen out of the sky or suffered an attack of amnesia, it's not likely you'll be honest-to-gosh hopelessly and entirely lost. Usually, if you get that sinking, stranger-in-the-woods feeling, you're just disoriented, not sure of your immediate surroundings. Yet by any other name it's still the same. When you don't know where you are, for all intents and purposes you're lost. Then what?

First of all, remain calm. Stop whatever you're doing. Sit down. Take a few deep breaths and relax until that sinking feeling subsides. Assure yourself that you can't be far from familiar territory.

Can you retrace your steps to the last place you knew where you were? If not, get out map and compass, which you *will* have with you, along with your

Some wilderness trails are clearly marked with signs installed by Park Rangers. Other trails are indicated by piled-up rocks (called "ducks") stacked by other backpackers.

essentials kit. Orient the map. On it spot the last point where you confirmed your location. On the map, and in your surroundings, look for identifiable landmarks such as prominent peaks, ridges, or drainage gullies. For a better view of the countryside, climb a tree, taking map and compass with you. Matching up map and landscape is usually all you'll need to do to find out where you are.

If that doesn't work, mark the spot where you are with a couple of rocks or a broken branch, so you'll recognize "home base" again, and—*keeping your gear with you*—walk in one direction for a hundred feet or so. If things don't look familiar, return to home base and walk in another direction. Continue to take straight-line excursions like spokes radiating out from a wheel hub. More often than not you'll intercept the trail or spot familiar ground.

If that doesn't work, signal for help. Blow a whistle, shout, or beat on your mess kit (a series of three signals means "Help!"). If hiking companions aren't too far away, they'll zero in on the noise.

If that doesn't work, resign yourself to staying put for a while, perhaps overnight. Find a protected spot and make a shelter. Set up tarp or tent, if you have your full pack; otherwise pile rocks or use tree branches to create a windbreak. If it's safe to do so, build a fire for warmth and for a signal.

Mark the area to help searchers, using rocks, articles of clothing, a brightly colored tarp or poncho, letters tramped in snow. Ration your food and water.

In cold weather it's essential that you stay out of the wind, sheltering in tent or tarp, rocks, trees, a natural cave, a snow cave. Keep yourself warm, especially your head, hands, and feet. Insulate yourself from snow with a ground pad, your pack, a climbing rope, tree branches. Put on dry socks and dry mittens. Wiggle your toes and fingers to discourage frostbite. Put your hands under your armpits, your feet inside a pack or in the crotch of a companion. Put on all the clothing you have. Get into a sleeping bag.

In desert heat, stay in whatever shade you can find or make with a shelter or clothing. Scrape away the top layer of hot sand to the cooler layer beneath. Avoid exhaustion and overheating. If you must travel, do it only at night, using a compass or stars for guidance. Drink plenty of liquid.

If statistics are at all comforting, most backpackers seldom become lost, and the few that do don't stay lost for very long. They find themselves in short order, or are found by searchers within a day or two. Of course, if before heading into the wild you left word or registered at a ranger station, your chances of being found quickly are excellent. But think of that before you leave, not after.

THE TRAVELER'S TERRAIN

People who believed the earth was flat obviously never walked very far. It has lumps, bumps, holes, and bulges of all shapes and sizes. It also has rocks, sand, snow, water, mud, marsh, brush, and forest, all of which you are going to come to eventually, whether you walk on a trail or go cross-country. When the going really gets rough you can elect to hike around the potentially bad parts. Discretion is sometimes the better part of valor. But when there's no other way, plunge on, bold and fearless—but carefully.

Snow and talus slopes are common terrain in the mountains. Sure footing in either requires care.

Rocks, Mud, and Snow

Lots of little loose rocks on lower mountain slopes or along the edges of a glacier are known as scree, and hiking in scree can be purgatory. One step forward and two steps back is not uncommon, while your feet slip and sink in the stuff and it works its way inside your boots. (Volcanic ash and powdery soil are also insidious underfoot.) If at all possible, move up scree slopes on a diagonal, planting your feet firmly and keeping your weight over them.

Bigger rocks on mountainsides, collectively called talus, range in shape from flat plates the size of your boot to jagged-edge chunks as big as a car. Talus is often unstable, so plant each foot carefully, and when you make a move be sure you're balanced. Your first experience on talus may fill your head with visions of broken arms and crushed legs, but in no time at all you'll be hopping around like a mountain goat.

Hiking for any distance in sand or very soft soil is tiring because your boots sink in, causing considerable friction. About all you can do on this kind of surface is look for hard-packed areas and take your time. Nor are marshes and bogs the most delightful places for extensive hiking. They actually seem to suck your boots in, and lifting your feet is a struggle. On top of all that are mosquitoes and other buzzing things. If there's no way around marshy land, look for grass-covered hummocks and hop across these bits of high ground.

Rain usually means mud, and mud can be very slick underfoot, even if you're wearing lug soles. I once slithered and fell mightily on a muddy trail where, weighed down by a heavy pack, I struggled like a turtle on its back. In order to get up I had to roll over on my stomach, which coated me nicely front and rear. At such times a hiking staff might help.

Deep, powdery snow? You shouldn't be in it unless you're wearing skis or snowshoes. In packed snow, kick steps when the slope steepens. On crusted snow be prepared in case you break through. Stay off steep ice unless you're wearing crampons. On flat ice, walk very carefully.

Stream Crossings

Unless you can step easily from bank to bank to get over a stream, spend a little time looking for a safe crossing. Any submerged rocks, even those less than an inch below the surface, are not safe, as they are often coated with a thin layer of algae that makes them slippery as sin. Large, dry rocks are best, if they are stable. A dry, solid tree trunk fallen across a watercourse can serve as a bridge. Again, a hiking staff or long stick makes a good third leg. If the thought of walking across a log spooks you, straddle it, sitting down, and inch your way over.

Sometimes you won't find a dry crossing over a gentle stream and will have to get your feet wet. If you have sneakers in your pack, wade over in them, changing back to dry socks and boots on the other side. No sneakers? Then slosh over in your boots and squelch along until they dry. It's better than chancing the crossing in bare feet and cutting yourself on a sharp stone. Also, cold mountain streams can numb bare feet in a jiffy.

Try to cross glacial runoffs and snowmelts in the morning when they are but trickles. By late afternoon the day's warmth may turn them into raging torrents, definitely not fit for wading.

Groups of hikers should pair up to wade fast-moving water. One person stays a couple of feet downstream, holding the other person securely as both move across the current. Thus, the downstream partner supports the upstream partner, who is taking the full force of the water for them both.

If a rope is available, the stronger hiker ties in to one end and wades across while the other pays out line, ready to haul in if need be. Once safely on the far shore, the leader brings the second hiker over. If several people must cross, the leader takes the rope end over and ties it to a tree or boulder on the far shore. The rope is then also anchored on the near shore to form a lifeline, which

Mountain streams swollen by late-afternoon snowmelt can be very hazardous, so don't take risks in crossing. Look for stable dry rocks or a sturdy log bridge. Unfasten your waist strap so you can get out of the pack fast if you tumble into the water.

everyone hangs onto as they wade over. The last person removes the rope and ties in to it to cross.

A fall into a shallow stream may hurt nothing more than your dignity, but tumbling into fast or deep water can be disastrous. Before starting a crossing, put loose gear inside your pack and secure all closures. *Unfasten the waist strap of your backpack.* If you fall, get out of the pack fast before it drags you under.

Bush and Brush

Look closely at a topographical map. Do you see any areas of little green dots, irregularly spaced? Those dots represent some of the most heartbreaking natural growth a backpacker has to face when venturing off a trail. Called scrub, brush, or chaparral, it's bushy stuff, anywhere from three to five feet high. Usually you can see over it, but trying to make your way through it is sheer hell. If you attempt to push it aside, it resists, grabbing at your legs and tripping up your feet. You get scratched, hot, tired, and cranky and expend a lot of energy without moving very far. Whenever possible, travel *around* scrub.

THE TRAVELER'S WEATHER

Neither rain, snow, nor sleet used to deter the postal service, but such natural elements can put a real damper on your backpacking trip unless you're able to cope with them. Coping with wilderness weather is a threefold business that involves being prepared for any eventuality, reading natural signs, and doing the right things at the right time. As in scouting, the key to all three is being prepared.

Being Prepared

Being prepared is realizing that not every day in the backcountry is sunshine and sparkling skies. When the weather is fine, enjoy it to the hilt, but don't assume it's going to be dry and clear for the entire trip. An all-day drizzle or sudden snow flurry should come as a matter of course, not a surprise.

Being prepared is outfitting yourself properly. A pack cover will keep your equipment from being soaked on the trail; rain gear will protect you while walking. For overnight protection—or if you have to lie low for a day—you'll have your tarp or tent.

Windbreaker, sweater, extra socks, and those other clothing items on your equipment list will keep you dry and warm, but only if they're with you. In the closet at home they won't be much help.

Reading Natural Signs

One of the skills every backpacker should acquire is the ability to read natural signs that tell of changing weather. You can make reasonably accurate short-range weather forecasts merely by observing cloud and wind patterns and by paying attention to matters closer to the ground. The indicators that follow are valid for most of the United States, including Alaska. In other parts of the world, weather patterns are different.

In mountainous areas a pattern of impending foul weather usually begins with the appearance of streaky clouds high up in the sky. So thin are these "mare's tails" that they don't really break the sunshine. If these wisps disappear and the sky stays blue, the weather will remain fair. But if they blend into a continuous whitish sheet or an overall rippled pattern, you can expect the possibility of rain within twenty-four hours. When the sky is sheeted over, the sun or moon may be surrounded by a fuzzy halo, another indicator of coming wet weather.

With the thickening and darkening of the sky from whitish to gray, sometimes in a wavy "buttermilk" pattern that blocks out the sun, comes the near certainty of a long, steady rain beginning within six hours. And if an accompanying wind kicks up from the south, reach for your foul-weather gear.

Any of these cloud types by itself isn't necessarily a forerunner of dirty weather, but in the mountains the sequence of development from one pattern to another is a good indication that wet is on the way.

Also watch for a Frisbee-shaped cloud cap on top of or near mountain peaks. If it grows, bad weather is on the way. If it shrinks, take heart, for you can expect fair weather.

Cloud patterns differ somewhat in plains and desert areas. There, big fluffy clouds that become darker and look angry usually indicate a change from fair weather to foul.

Some other natural signs? If the atmosphere becomes crystal clear and the air has a fresh smell, a storm may be approaching. Insects and birds may stay close to the ground. Wildflowers may close up. Smoke may rise a little way, then flatten out or sink closer to the ground.

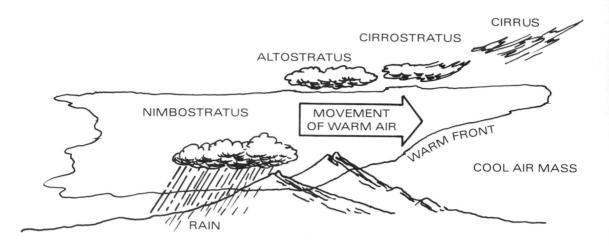

CROSS-SECTION THROUGH A WARM FRONT

A vertical cross-section through a warm front pressure system shows how warm air replaces relatively cooler air. A cloud sequence beginning with streaky, high cirrus, then a continuous sheet of cirrostratus, followed by thick, dark altostratus, means rain-bearing nimbostratus is likely. The wet weather may last eight to twenty-four hours or, if several systems are linked together, hang on for several days.

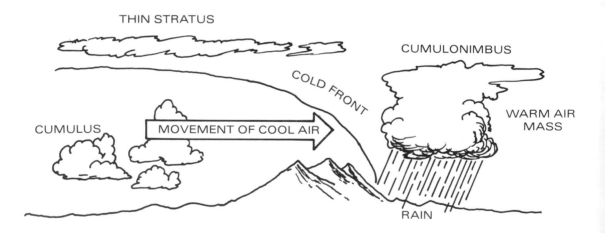

CROSS-SECTION THROUGH A COLD FRONT

A cold front is a surface along which cold air replaces relatively warmer air. Anvil-shaped cumulonimbus clouds moving in from the west or northwest usually bring violent thunderstorm activity, followed by rain, hail, or snow. Such weather may last two to five hours, but it will be followed by several days of clear weather.

In either mountains or desert, if a warm wind starts blowing from the south and low, dark clouds cover the sky, prepare for bad weather.

Doing the Right Things

So you're loaded with all the right equipment, and you've watched clouds until your neck is stiff, and the wind is snapping at your heels, and you know that before long things are going to bust loose (or maybe rain is already pouring down). Then what?

If you're on the move, get into your rain gear and cover your pack. Walk slowly so you don't become overheated and drenched with perspiration. Look for a place where you can settle in for the night, or at least until the weather blows over. If you want to wait things out, get under a leafy tree, spread a tarp, or just sit in your rain gear and try not to be too miserable.

Of course, if you want to keep moving and are well protected, go right ahead. Hiking in rain can be a delightful experience as long as you keep dry.

If you elect to make camp in the rain, don't stand around analyzing the situation or discussing the weather with companions. You already know it's

When making camp in miserable weather, the first order of business is pitching a shelter. You must keep yourself and your equipment dry.

raining; what you want to do is get under cover. Set up shelter immediately, and go under or into it. Take off your wet things and put on dry clothing. If everything is soaked you may have to build a fire to help matters along. (See How to Build a Fire in chapter 7.)

While rain is pelting down, stay sheltered as much as possible so you'll remain dry. Tent-bound, you can talk, sing songs, play cards, read, write, mend clothing, sleep, or just be lulled by the soothing sound of rain pattering on your shelter.

When you're out in wintry weather, periodically brush snow off your jacket, pants, and boot tops before it has a chance to melt. Wiggle your toes and fingers to encourage circulation. In your shelter, bundle up in clothing or snuggle into your sleeping bag to stay warm.

Because too much exertion in hot weather can bring on heat exhaustion, many experienced backpackers "go to ground" when the temperature rises into the nineties. If you too believe that only mad dogs and Englishmen go out in the noonday sun, find some shade, shuck off your pack, and relax until the world cools down. If you choose to keep moving, slow your pace and, in the sun, keep your head covered. Take frequent rest stops, and drink plenty of fluids.

When skies lower or thunderheads build, be prepared for lightning. A real hazard, especially in high country, lightning goes for objects that stick up prominently, whether they be peaks, ridges, hilltops, or you.

When a storm threatens and you're just above timberline, move back down into the woods, staying away from single tall trees, which may act as lightning rods. If you can't reach a patch of forest, at least don't present a good target. Get off summits and ridges into gullies or saddles. Stay away from overhangs and caves, where lethal electrical currents may run.

If lightning starts zapping near you, don't panic. Put some distance between you and major metal objects, such as crampons or an ice ax. Throw down your pack, sit on it to insulate yourself from the ground, pull both feet up, and hug your knees close to your chest until the fireworks are over.

An ideal campsite should be flat, protected from prevailing winds, receive early morning sun, and have a good water source nearby.

Settling and Sheltering

With full pack on your weary back you're way out in the woods, too far from home or the nearest motel to make it back before nightfall, and soon night will be falling. It's time to think about settling and sheltering.

Maybe Hansel and Gretel just stumbled into a place to bed down, but look what almost happened to them. To avoid a similar situation you should start looking for a campsite at least an hour before dusk so you can be settled, sheltered, and fed before dark. Overnight stays should be planned; they shouldn't just happen. Rigging a shelter in blackness is one of backpacking's lesser experiences.

CAMPSITE CONSIDERATIONS

In choosing a place to bed down, one of your first considerations should be safety. Avoid sites at the base of barren, steep slopes that could be swept by avalanches or scoured by falling rocks. Beware of camping near dead trees that could snap and topple in a wind, or sleeping under snow-laden branches that could dump their load on your shelter.

Ideally, bedding-down ground should be flat.

139

Even with a candle lantern suspended from a tree branch, a campsite can have minimum impact on the environment.

A mild slope can be okay as long as you sleep with your head higher than your feet (the other way around may give you a fierce headache). But on any real incline you'll be fighting all night to keep from sliding downhill.

Try to pick a site that isn't buffeted by prevailing winds, or else look for natural shelters and windbreaks, such as brush, trees, or boulders. Avoid meadows and marshes, which suffer most from human impact (besides, the mosquitoes were there first), and make sure you aren't in a natural drainage area that could be filled with a torrent in a rainfall.

Recognize and avail yourself of microclimates—local temperature and wind variations created by topography. At night, hilltops and rises can be warmer than nearby low areas. Cold air tends to flow down gullies and settle in valleys.

Consider the sun exposure of a potential site. If you have a choice of late afternoon sun or early morning sun, choose the spot that receives early morning sun. It'll help thaw your bones and dry your sleeping bag.

Ideally, a water source should be nearby, but in a pinch a full canteen will see you through a night. On the other hand, try to avoid camping at the water's edge, which can hasten bank erosion and disturb the watering habits of wildlife.

Another place *not* to camp is on or near a trail. Other hikers don't want to see your camp, and you certainly don't want to be disturbed by passersby.

Groups of backpackers should keep plenty of space between them when bedding down, not only for privacy but to minimize their impact on the land. A group's presence can also be felt by other nearby campers, so when you

High-altitude camps in some heavily used hiking areas may have low rock walls to protect individual sites from buffeting winds.

socialize with fellow travelers, keep the noise down. And it's common courtesy not to make your camp right next to someone who was there first.

In the interest of reducing human impact on the land, here are a few more don'ts regarding your campsites: Don't dig trenches around sleeping areas (instead, choose a spot that water won't puddle up in or wash over). Don't cut off or pull down tree branches, even dead ones. Don't move large rocks or logs. Don't build wind shelters with stones unless you plan to dismantle them later. Don't drive nails into trees to anchor guy lines. Don't leave broken guy lines lying around or attached to trees when you break camp.

SETTING UP CAMP

Every experienced backpacker has his or her own procedure for setting up camp, based on personal values. Those with the hungries establish their cooking/eating area first. Comfort lovers hunt for the ideal sleeping site. Bladder-and-bowel hikers mark off the latrine. Of course, if rain is falling or darkness is imminent, shelter comes first. Under normal conditions (dry weather, plenty of light), my unvarying ritual after finding a likely site is as follows:

Leaning my pack against an accommodating tree or rock, I give the ground a visual sweep, picturing myself in complete repose. If fair weather seems a safe bet, only a groundsheet-sized area is needed; otherwise I allow for shelter staking and guying. Finding the ideal level spot, I crawl around on hands and knees, picking and patting at the earth to remove small rocks, sticks, prickly leaves, and other sleep-disturbing objects. Sometimes I lie flat to make sure no lumps remain. Then I spread my ground cloth and erect a shelter over it, or else just fluff out my sleeping bag on it.

Next comes the kitchen. Out of the pack I dig stove, cooking gear, and food and group them next to a rock or log that can serve as a seat. If there's a chance of rain, I either stretch a tarp over the kitchen or plan to cook under my shelter. In bear country I look for a tree to hang edibles from.

Water is next. Filling canteens or water bag, I bring them back to the kitchen, where they'll be ready for meal preparation.

In all the wandering around I spot a place for a latrine, well away from camp, any water source, or a trail, and that completes my camp setup. Elapsed time, about half an hour.

Stringing a tarp between trees gives good wind and rain shelter for the camp kitchen area.

KEEPING FOOD SAFE

In the backcountry you are not the only creature interested in your food. With no qualms whatsoever, wildlife large and small will plunder your provisions if given half a chance. Sharing food, willingly or unwillingly, with woodsy critters is not in anybody's best interest. First, human food isn't good for wild animals (and it establishes habit patterns in them); second, you need your food more than they do.

Ants and other bugs will find a way to almost anything edible left on the ground for long, even though it's wrapped in plastic. So will mice, marmots, ground squirrels, pikas, chipmunks, raccoons, and other pawing, gnawing critters. Most of these furry fellows will crawl right into a pack or else chew their way into it to reach the goodies. The best way to foil them at their game is to

144

suspend all food—including candy and gum—from a tree branch. Either leave it in your backpack and haul up the whole works or, better yet, pack food in its own stuff sack so it can be kept separate from other gear.

The game has a different set of rules in bear country. Especially in National Parks, bears assume that helping themselves to human food is their God-given right, and you must take certain precautions to protect your comestibles from them.

Any time you leave camp for more than a few minutes, and at night, hang all food from a tree branch in a sealed plastic bag. But not just any old limb. Look for a sturdy horizontal branch 15 to 20 feet off the ground. Tie a rock to one end of a nylon cord and toss the rock over the branch, 5 to 10 feet out from the trunk. Now tie your sealed food bag to the cord's other end and haul it high until it hangs about 6 feet below the branch. Then run the hauling line diagonally and secure it to another tree or a large rock. When you need supplies, just lower the bag.

Some bear experts claim the woods are full of really wise bruins that have this diagonal-line technique all figured out and know just how to break the anchor line to drop the goodies. These experts say the only way to bear-proof food is to plastic-bag it, tie a short (10- to 20-foot) length of cord between the food bag and a rock-in-a-bag counterbalance, hang everything over a limb that's 15 or 20 feet up, and then push the counterbalance up with a stick until both it and the food bag are at least 10 feet off the ground. To retrieve your food,

To get at food, bears will destroy anything, including stuff sacks, backpacks, or tents.

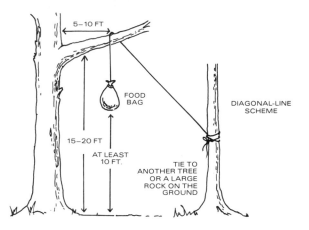

5–10 FT

FOOD
BAG

DIAGONAL-LINE
SCHEME

15–20 FT

AT LEAST
10 FT.

TIE TO
ANOTHER TREE
OR A LARGE
ROCK ON THE
GROUND

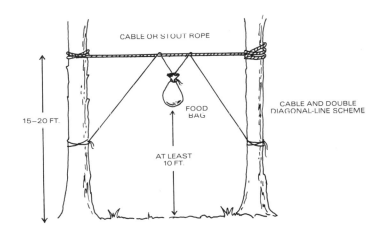

CABLE OR STOUT ROPE

CABLE AND DOUBLE
DIAGONAL-LINE SCHEME

FOOD
BAG

15–20 FT.

AT LEAST
10 FT.

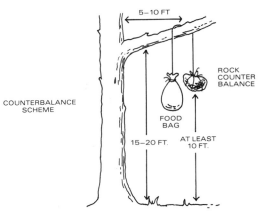

5–10 FT

ROCK
COUNTER
BALANCE

COUNTERBALANCE
SCHEME

FOOD
BAG

15–20 FT.

AT LEAST
10 FT.

To keep bears and smaller animals
from your food, seal all edibles in a
plastic bag and hang it high by slinging
a line over a tree branch or a cable.

push the counterbalance higher until the food bag comes down to where you can reach it.

It's a good method, as long as you don't lose or break your pushing stick. Some park campgrounds even have steel cables stretched between trees for the purpose. Rangers advise the cable-and-counterbalance scheme or else a double-diagonal hauling line (in case one is broken by Bruin).

These operations may seem a nuisance to go through every night, but if a bear snaffles your food in the middle of a two-week trek, you could be in big trouble.

ABOUT LIGHTWEIGHT SHELTERS

As often as possible I retire under the open heavens, gazing at the sparkling stars until I doze off. There's a spell in the night sky that enhances the feeling of oneness with nature. And there's indescribable magic in being wakened by the light of a full moon, a luminescence so bright you can read a book by it.

To generalize wildly, most of the time in most places I can sleep under the stars, with nothing between my eyes and them except perhaps a leafy tree branch to ward off the night damp. However, dew and fog can wet a sleeping bag, so sometimes I bed down inside a bivouac sack.

A bivouac sack encloses a sleeping bag from top to bottom, giving protection from night damp or even a drizzle. Although most water-repellent bivouac sacks keep water off the outside of a sleeping bag, they cause condensation inside, and you still wake up clammy. On the other hand, a Gore-Tex bivvy sack repels water while allowing inside vapor to escape. As a matter of course, I carry my ground cloth, sleeping pad, and bivvy sack all rolled up together. If dry weather seems promising, I unroll all this and shake out my sleeping bag on top of it. If wetness is in the air, I poke the sleeping bag down inside the sack. Even in a light rain I stay dry.

A bivvy sack does hold in body heat, which is a real plus on a cold night. However, on a warm night you may be too warm in one.

For greater protection—or if you just like the feeling of having a shelter over your body—consider the versatile tarp. Using guy lines, a pair of tent poles, and a few stakes, you are limited only by your imagination as to the ways you can rig a good tarp ("good" meaning made of coated nylon, grommeted along the edges). With a roomy ground cloth under a sizable tarp, you and a couple of companions can stay dry even in a steady rain.

Plastic sheets are of limited use as tarps. True, they shed rain, but they are

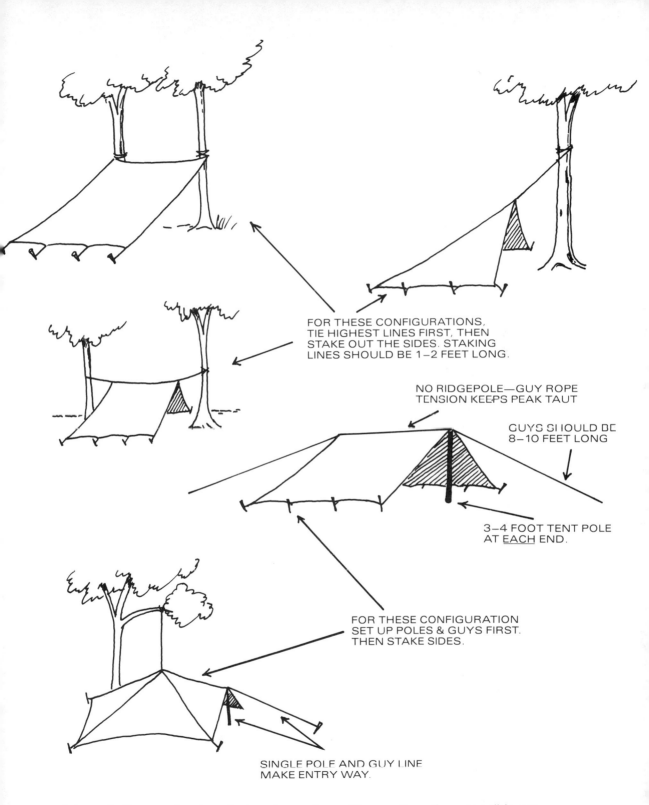

FOR THESE CONFIGURATIONS,
TIE HIGHEST LINES FIRST, THEN
STAKE OUT THE SIDES. STAKING
LINES SHOULD BE 1–2 FEET LONG.

NO RIDGEPOLE—GUY ROPE
TENSION KEEPS PEAK TAUT

GUYS SHOULD BE
8–10 FEET LONG

3–4 FOOT TENT POLE
AT EACH END.

FOR THESE CONFIGURATION
SET UP POLES & GUYS FIRST.
THEN STAKE SIDES.

SINGLE POLE AND GUY LINE
MAKE ENTRY WAY.

A tarp shelter can be rigged almost anywhere. The configurations possible are
limited only by your ingenuity.

A securely rigged tarp makes a good
sunshade and will protect you from
even a heavy downpour. Trees, brush,
or rocks make good anchor points, and
a pair of tent poles provides added
versatility.

bulky and tear easily. The same goes for the so-called tube tent, which isn't really a tent at all. An open-ended plastic or coated-nylon sleeve, it's easily rigged by running a line through it and tying the line between two trees. In theory—and low price—a tube tent is fine, but in practice it leaves a lot to be desired. First, it's fragile. Second, being completely waterproof it causes condensation inside, despite its open ends. And, third, if rain starts falling, these open ends are like two end-to-end funnels with you in between.

It's possible to rig a poncho as a shelter, but the small size limits its usefulness. If you do use a poncho, remember to close the head hole.

ABOUT TENTS

Tarps can be strung in rather exotic ways to withstand quite a bit of even wind-driven rain, but when the weather really gets nasty, or snow starts flying, or bugs become thick, a tent is a must. If you've always associated tents with those huge canvas and rope affairs that hold a family of four, plus dog, and require brute force for setting up, you'll be delighted with the lightweight shelters developed for backpacking. You may also feel somewhat intimidated by the variety of shapes, styles, sizes, and types of tents available. To keep things simple, let's start with the premise that virtually every tent has a floor, walls (also called canopy), and supporting framework.

Function and Design

The functions of a tent are to keep you dry, warm, and bug-free. A large plastic bag will do all that, so why go to the expense of buying a tent? How does a good tent differ from a plastic bag?

Aside from shape, the greatest difference is in venting. A plastic bag won't eliminate water vapor, whereas a well-designed tent will. In a single night, between perspiration, exhalation, and evaporation from wet clothing, the human body may produce more than a pint of water in the form of vapor. If that water isn't carried off, it will transform the inside of a tent into a swamp.

Most well-designed tents have small openings—called vents—at each end, close to the ridge. Vents encourage air circulation, which flushes out warm, moisture-laden atmosphere. Vents also bring in fresh air to replace carbon dioxide exhaled from the lungs.

To further encourage the escape of vapor, the main canopy of a tent is most often made of breathable nylon. To keep rain from seeping in, a waterproof rain

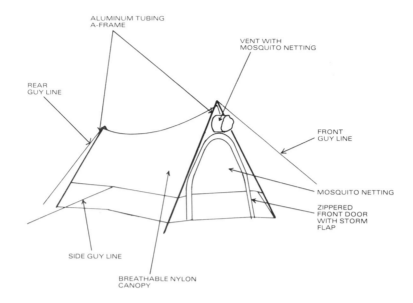

ALUMINUM TUBING
A-FRAME

VENT WITH
MOSQUITO NETTING

REAR
GUY LINE

FRONT
GUY LINE

MOSQUITO NETTING

ZIPPERED
FRONT DOOR
WITH STORM
FLAP

SIDE GUY LINE

BREATHABLE NYLON
CANOPY

The basic A-frame or wedge tent is a favorite of many backpackers. Relatively simple to set up, it's very stable in windy weather.

fly is fitted over the canopy. A tent can be set up without its rain fly and used strictly for wind and insect shelter. Then if rain starts falling, the fly can be rigged in a jiffy. A fly should be taut enough that it doesn't touch the canopy. If it does, leaks will develop.

A double-walled tent has an integral rain fly that goes up when the tent is pitched.

Most tents have a zippered doorway that can be opened partially or fully, usually backed up by a separately zippered insect screen. A tunnel entrance is commonly used on winter tents. It's a loose sleeve that is rolled and tied open, or closed with a drawstring.

A vestibule is an extension of the canopy beyond the tent's entrance, forming a kind of protected "porch." Some tents have vestibules, some don't. The extra covered space is handy for stowing your pack or shoes rather than crowding them inside the tent. It also makes a dandy kitchen when bad weather keeps you under cover.

A good tent floor should be completely waterproof and, to exclude ground

Providing extra space for shoes and other gear, a tent vestibule also gives you dressing room.

moisture, should extend several inches up the sides and ends of the canopy. Tent floors usually have seams, but the better ones have no perimeter seams, which are the most susceptible to leakage.

Basic Tent Forms

The most widely used type of backpacking tent is the basic A-frame or wedge. At each end of this tent a pair of poles join at the top, forming an inverted V. Floor and walls are supported by the V pairs, which are usually held apart by guy lines. Stakes hold the floor flat. The A-frame is very stable in strong winds, it sheds rain and snow quite well, and it is relatively easy to set up. The A-frame is a longtime favorite of many experienced backpackers.

An I-pole tent is similar in shape to the wedge, only its support is simpler. Instead of a pair of slanted poles, it has a single vertical pole at each end. An I-pole tent can be set up and taken down more quickly than an A-frame, but an I-pole requires more guying and is not as stable. Also, because the vertical poles obstruct the entrance, you sometimes knock them askew crawling in and out.

A tepee or pyramid tent has either a single center pole or several side poles joined at one end to form an apex from which the walls are draped. It's a very stable design, and the steeply sloping walls do an excellent job of shedding rain and snow. But setting up a tepee is sometimes a two-person operation.

A slight drawback inherent to such sloping tents is the limited headroom, except in the center. Also, in order for their sides to be taut, most tepees must be guyed and staked. If you're grounded by incessant rain, sitting yoga-fashion in the middle of a tent, perhaps facing your partner who is sitting the same way, can quickly grow stale.

Most backpackers don't mind pounding a few stakes, but those who are dead set against monkeying around with pegs and guy lines find the answer in a freestanding tent. A series of flexible tubes or rods form a freestanding tent's framework, which holds floor and walls taut by its springy tension. Freestanding designs, such as domes, tunnels, and certain exterior-frame configurations, hold their shape without staking or guying (though in very strong winds, some staking may be necessary to keep the whole works from being blown away). When erected, freestanding tents can be picked up and moved. Because of their near-vertical walls, you can sit almost anywhere inside without rounding your shoulders or crooking your neck.

A semi-freestanding tent has flexible poles to hold the canopy taut and requires only two stakes.

A freestanding "dome" tent can be cleaned out simply by picking it up and turning it upside down. Except in high winds, freestanding tents don't require staking.

Types of Tents

There are backpacking tents, and there are backpacking tents. Some are designed to protect you from mosquitoes; others are designed to protect you from everything short of a cataclysm. Not all types are readily available everywhere, and the names may vary from one geographical region to another. But to understand your options, you should know something about the various types on the market.

Summer Tents

Summer tents include such subcategories as forest tents, net tents, rain tents, desert tents, and tropical tents. Also called one-season tents, they are intended for use in temperate climates where bugs and rain are the primary concern. Summer tents are extremely lightweight and have plenty of insect netting, which gives added venting.

Three-season Tents

These supposedly take you through spring, summer, and fall. Somewhat sturdier than strictly summer tents, they have less insect netting and can withstand considerable wind without collapsing or flying away with you inside. Three-season tents are sometimes known as mountaineering tents.

Winter Tents

Also called expedition tents, arctic tents, or high-altitude tents, winter tents are the sturdiest of all. They can, of course, be used anywhere, any time, but if you pitch an expedition tent on a Florida beach you're guilty of overkill and will probably be laughed into the Everglades. Some winter tents have a skirt of material extending out from the floor on which rock or snow is piled to anchor the tent against gales. These snow flaps add extra weight, but sometimes they work better than stakes.

A winter tent should have an entry at each end in case one end is buried in snow. Many winter tents have a frost liner, a detachable inner canopy which absorbs moisture that might otherwise freeze on the inside of the regular canopy.

Hardware and Accessories

If your shelter is a tarp, you can choose from several types of tent poles. If you buy a tent, you haven't any choice unless you want to replace the supplied poles with something else.

The best tent poles are hollow fiberglass or aluminum tubing sections that are smaller at one end than the other. Fitted together to whatever length is needed, they will support a shelter with very little wobble.

The handiest tent poles are shock-corded. A length of stout elastic cord runs through the hollow sections, keeping them together when stored and snapping them into locked position when needed. Freestanding tents have slim, flexible poles or wands.

The least expensive tent pole is a solid wood affair that looks like a jointed broomstick. Unless you have no other options, steer clear of wooden poles. They are heavy and not very stable.

Guy lines are lengths of strong cord—usually braided nylon—that you run from tent or tarp to some kind of anchor (stake, tree, rock) to stabilize the shelter. After pitching a shelter a couple of times, you'll know what length guy lines it needs. Make them up and leave them tied to the shelter so you don't have to fiddle around securing them each time you set up camp.

Tighten and secure a guy line by looping it around an anchor and tying the loose end around the taut part with a slip knot. Or use store-bought tighteners—small pieces of notched plastic or drilled metal that hold a line tight by friction.

Because you won't always find rocks and trees handy to use as anchors, you should carry a set of stakes, including a couple of spares. Wooden pegs may be fine for the family's big canvas tent, but, like wooden poles, they're much

So simple a child can handle them, tent pole sections held together with elastic shock cords fit together quickly and are seldom misplaced.

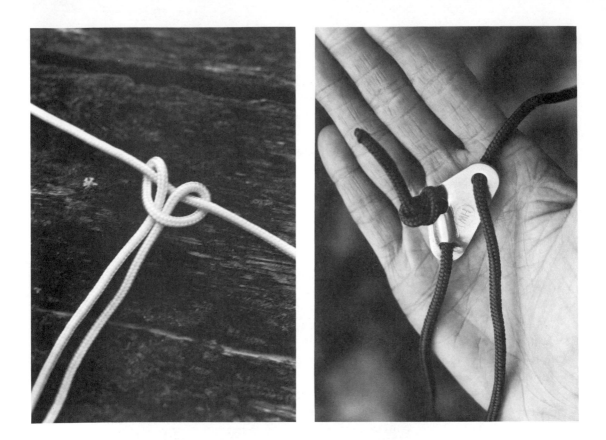

Secure a guy line by looping it around an anchor and tying it back on itself with a tight sliding knot, or else use a store-bought tightener.

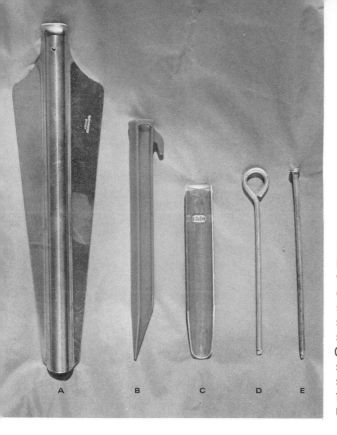

Because tent stakes vary greatly in form and function, you may want to carry two or more different kinds. A: Wide aluminum stake suitable for deep snow or soft sand. B: High-impact plastic stake for compacted earth. C: U-section aluminum stake for sand, loose earth, and compacted snow. D: Aluminum skewer for firm earth. E: Aluminum spike for rocky ground.

too bulky for backpacking. Wide plastic pegs or U-section aluminum stakes are best in sand, loose earth, and snow (but if the snow is really soft you may have to tie the stakes crosswise and bury them). Aluminum skewers and staples work well in firm ground. In rocky places use aluminum spikes.

To ensure water repellency, tent and tarp seams must be sealed. A few manufacturers do this and include their labor costs in the price, but most supply the sealer and let you do the job. It's no big deal. Just set up the tent and apply sealer according to the instructions on the label. Let the seams dry twice as long as the label says so they won't stick together when you stow the shelter.

Picking a Tent

Find yourself obsessed with the notion of purchasing a tent? Stop a moment to ask yourself if you really need to own one. If you're strictly a fair-weather backpacker, you probably don't need any more shelter than a spreading tree branch, plus a lightweight tarp for emergencies. If you expect fogs, infrequent drizzles, or light showers, a tarp or bivvy sack will probably suffice. But if you really want bug, rain, or snow protection, perhaps the best way to go is with a tent.

As with most other equipment, take your time. Don't let eagerness to snuggle down in your own little cocoon cause you to make a hasty decision or to overbuy. Remember, the more tent you choose, usually the more dollars come out of your pocket and the more pounds go on your back.

Try before you buy. Borrow or rent, experimenting with more than one style, more than one shape, to find out which suits you best. Determine which form and which type answers your needs and has the most features desirable to you. Because no one tent has everything, the name of the game is compromise —not compromise in quality but in what you want from a shelter. Following are a few questions to ask yourself as you look and learn.

What size tent do you require? What type of tent (A-frame, I-pole, tepee, freestanding) best meets your needs? Is pitching a one-person operation, or will you require seven hands to set things up in a nagging wind? How many stakes must be used? How much does the tent weigh? Or, more to the point, how much shelter weight are you willing to carry? Will the venting permit good cross-ventilation?

Check seams. The best tent seams are flat-fell. This means fabric edges are not just laid atop one another but are folded over so the stitching passes through four layers of material, resulting in greater strength and better water-shedding capability.

Check stitching. Stitching everywhere should be even and tight, with no loose loops of thread. Stress points should be reinforced. Attachments for grommets, stake loops, guy lines, and zippers must be capable of handling strain without pulling loose, so inspect them carefully.

Zippers should operate easily from outside as well as inside, and they should have storm flaps or some other protection against wind-driven rain and insects.

When properly pitched, a tent should stand proudly, unsagging, unwrinkled. A tent that looks like a pair of baggy pants, even after you've done everything right in setting it up, has something wrong with it, and even though it may keep rain off you, it will probably flap maddeningly in a wind.

Ask the salesperson to knock down and set up the demonstrator model at least once so you can learn about any tricky maneuvers. And no matter how good a demonstrator model looks in the store, inspect the tent you're purchasing before you take it home. Remove it from its box or sack and make sure you have all the hardware and parts you're entitled to—stakes, poles, guy lines, rain fly. Make sure seams are sealed, or that you have enough sealer to do the job yourself.

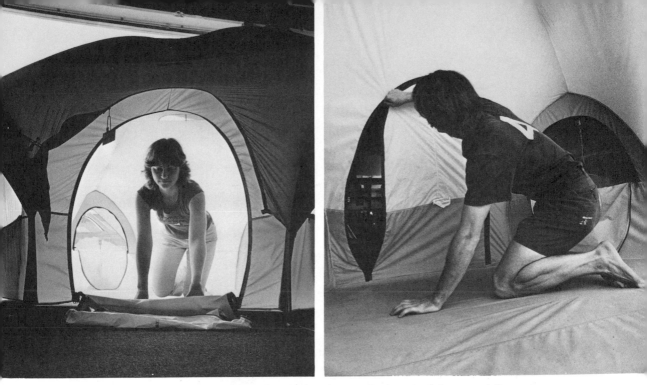

When shopping for a tent, get in and out of a demonstrator model several times, imagining yourself doing it in wind, rain, and snow. Check for good cross-ventilation. See if closures fit tightly. Try all zippers to make sure they work smoothly. And know how to set the tent up and take it down.

Pitching a Tent

Once you have a tent (or tarp) home—be it yours or someone else's—set it up and take it down a couple of times to get the hang of the operation. Better to fumble in your backyard than in the backcountry. Also, home is a good place to seal seams, secure guy lines to grommets, and in general check out accessories and hardware.

In siting a tent or tarp in the wild, try to find a spot that offers some natural shelter. If you have a choice, wooded areas give more wind protection than open spaces.

If the ground isn't too hard, you can push stakes in with the heel of your hand or your boot sole. Otherwise you may have to pound them gently with a rock—not too hard or they may bend. If stakes pull out of soft ground or sand, make "deadmen" by tying the guy lines around their middle and burying them crosswise to the main pull of the lines.

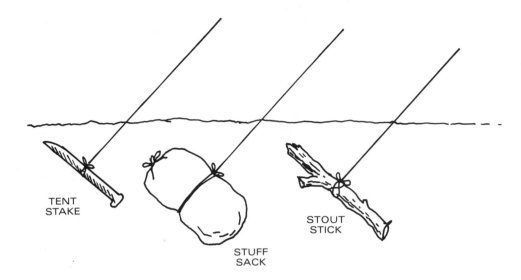

TENT
STAKE

STUFF
SACK

STOUT
STICK

If tent stakes won't hold in soft ground, sand, or snow, make a "deadman" by tying a guy line around a stake, stick, or stuff sack filled with soil, then burying it.

Pitching a tent on snow takes a little fussing around. First pack the snow firmly by stamping it down with skis, snowshoes, or boots. Again, if the stakes don't hold, make deadmen of them.

If the ground is too hard or rocky for stakes, you can guy from the rocks themselves or place a rock on top of a tied stake lying on the ground.

Sharing a shelter with another person? Unless your partner is really appealing, the two of you might want to sleep head-to-foot. Both parties gain a little more room, and snorers are a bit more isolated.

Tent Care

Before entering a tent, remove your shoes and leave them outside, or else put them in a plastic trash bag. Nothing messes up a floor quicker than tracked-in debris. When breaking down a tent, sweep out sand, leaves, and twigs, or turn the tent wrongside out and shake out such fabric-puncturing objects.

Allow a tent to air and dry inside and out before packing it, as trapped moisture will make it heavier and hasten its deterioration. If you must move on before your tent is thoroughly dry, set it up again as soon as possible to get rid of the dampness and let the seams dry.

Tents, tarps, and ground cloths should be stuffed into stuff sacks rather than being neatly folded or rolled. This may make the fabric look like unironed laundry, but it prevents the development of areas of wear along crease lines.

For emergency repairs, such as mending tiny punctures and small tears, carry a roll of adhesive nylon tape or other fabric mending tape. All logic and common sense say that sealed seams shouldn't leak, but sometimes in a downpour logic goes out the door and a seam may begin to drip. For on-the-spot relief, try rubbing the leaky point with lip balm, candle wax, or shoe sealant. Sounds weird, but it's been known to work for a while.

Keep your tent and sleeping gear clean by removing shoes before entering. In fair weather you can leave shoes outside; otherwise put them in a protective plastic bag and bring them in.

Cooking and Dining

I have an outdooring friend who tramps the back-country for days at a time, blissfully munching Brazil nuts and dried peaches that have been warmed in his pocket to body temperature. Another friend won't set foot on the trail without fresh vegetables, canned meats, herbs, and—so help me—a backpacker's pressure cooker. One a spartan, the other a sybarite, they are on opposite ends of the alfresco cooking and dining scale.

Though some hardy souls couldn't care less about camping cuisine, most of us take delight in the thought of a steaming pot of stew for dinner. And nothing starts a day quite like a cup of hot tea or cocoa.

WHEN TO BUILD A FIRE

As of this writing, microwave ovens and solar cookers haven't proved practical for backpackers. Therefore, hot food means fire. Fire in the woods can be bad on a couple of counts, for as Smokey Bear used to remind us, uncontrolled fires can destroy woods. Controlled fires can, too. They just take longer.

Every day more people are camping, which

164   means every day more twigs, branches, and whole trees are being broken up, cut down, and consumed in controlled campfires. That tree won't miss this dead branch, you say to yourself as you smash it down. Besides, you rationalize, burning it will tidy up the place and make the countryside look more natural.

Right? Wrong! If everyone goes around tidying up the backcountry by yanking dead branches off trees, trees will soon be bare and most *un*natural-looking. Dead branches are part of the landscape. Leave them on the trees. Let nature take care of them.

In the wilderness, fires are seldom needed for cooking, as mentioned in chapter 1. Bonfires usually are a creature comfort, an atavistic throwback to

"Are the socks done yet?" A campfire may be necessary to dry wet clothing or to keep you warm. But in the wilderness, build a fire only if you really need one.

our cave-dwelling days when a roaring blaze kept away beasts and warmed chilled bodies. Admittedly, a campfire can be cozy on a cool night, but not many beasts roam the forests anymore. And more often than not you can warm up by putting on a sweater or crawling into your sleeping bag.

When is a fire really necessary? Usually only in an emergency situation. If you can't get warm or dry any other way, build a fire. It may be your only means of survival.

WHERE TO BUILD A FIRE

If you must build a fire, use downed wood, wood that nature has dropped to the ground. Choose your site carefully, staying away from trails, streamsides, and lakeshores, where blackened fire rings are more likely to be seen by other hikers. Stick to bare ground, away from dry grass, brush, and overhead branches, all of which can carry a blaze to bigger things. Be mindful of how wind can whip sparks and scatter embers. Keep fires small. Roaring affairs with leaping flames are hard to control and really aren't necessary.

Don't build fires next to standing rocks or on soft, mossy ground. The first will retain sooty traces of your having been there; the second may smolder long after you've gone and eventually burst into flame.

HOW TO BUILD A FIRE

Before starting a fire, you should perform two operations that will save you time, and possibly trouble, later. First clear the immediate site of all burnable material by pushing away bits of wood, fallen leaves, decomposed plant material—anything on the forest floor that could be ignited by flames or embers. If you can, scrape down to bare earth. Next, so you don't have to leave the fire unattended while you go wood hunting, gather wood and stack it nearby but not too close to the site.

To get things going, crumple paper into a loose ball and place it on the ground. On top of the paper lay a handful of loose tinder, such as shredded bark, wood shavings, or dry splinters. Add kindling in the form of split sticks or dry twigs, arranging it in lean-to, tepee, or log-cabin fashion. In the same manner add a few larger pieces, placing them close enough together that fire can move from one to another, but not so close as to cut off air. If you pack things too tightly, all you'll get is smoke. If wood is wet, split small pieces or shave away outer layers to the dry inner parts.

Basic fire building requires starting with small twigs and working up to larger pieces of wood. Be sure to leave plenty of space for air circulation.

Now light the paper, shielding the match from wind until paper and kindling ignite. If the fire seems balky, blow on it or fan it gently at ground level to provide more air. Don't use stove fuel to start a fire. It will usually flare up and burn off quickly without really igniting the wood.

Unless you want to go primitive with flint and steel or rub sticks together, your basic fire starter is the humble match. Either book matches or wooden matches are fine, as long as you keep them dry—not just water-dry but damp-dry. Wet matches crumble before you can light them; damp matches sputter and go out. Keep matches dry by storing them in an airtight container or wrapping them in plastic.

Cigarette lighters work just as well as matches but require flints and fuel. And it always seems that such handy gadgets fail when you need them most.

Several products on the market—such as tablets, blocks, pastes, and jellies—are called fire starters but actually are solid fuels that must be ignited with a match before they'll burn. Some backpackers prefer them (or a candle stub) to paper, which isn't always available on a backcountry trek.

A final word regarding fires: In extinguishing a fire, make sure it's out, out, out. Douse the ashes with water. Spread them apart and douse them again. Then douse them once more for good measure. Finally, work them into the soil and sweep the area with a stick or your shoe so no one can ever tell you've been there.

When leaving a campfire site, douse the ashes several times with water, then work them into the soil to eliminate all traces of your having been there.

ABOUT STOVES

If you appreciate efficiency in little packages, you'll be captivated by backpacking stoves. Compact, lightweight, and marvelously simple, they are designed to function with a minimum of fuss and bother on your part. But remember, a stove is to cook. Sometimes you need to cook, sometimes you don't. When you do, the stove had better work and work well or all its cleverness will be of absolutely no value.

Stove Fuels

The basic function of a backpacking stove is to raise the temperature of water to the boiling point. This it does through combustion of man-made fuel. Stove and fuel: two more objects to add to your pack. Let's look at fuels first.

White Gasoline and Kerosene

Perhaps the most commonly used backpacking stove fuel in North America, white gasoline is a highly volatile, additive-free version of automobile gasoline. Easily ignited, it burns clean and hot. Unlike automobile gasoline (which will gum up a stove), white gas is not sold at every corner service station. Some, but not all, hardware stores carry it. Most users of white gas stoves use a substitute called "camp stove fuel" or "Coleman fuel." Less volatile, it also lights easily and burns fast. And it's available in most backpacking shops, sporting goods stores, and hardware stores.

Kerosene is less volatile than white gas, which means it doesn't ignite as easily (a drawback when you're trying to get a stove going with fingers numb with cold). Also, kerosene stains almost any fabric it touches, and the smell permeates clothing, sleeping bags, and packs. It is difficult to start, and it may smoke. But on the positive side, kerosene is available almost anywhere in the world, it burns hotter than white gas, and it's much safer to use.

To start a white gas stove you simply prime it with a little of its own fuel. Light the fuel with a match, wait a few seconds, then turn on the burner. If the parts are reasonably clean, the stove will usually come to life with no fuss. A kerosene stove can be more temperamental. It usually has to be pumped up to pressure, then primed with alcohol or solid fuel (something else to carry), then ignited. If you rush the ritual, the stove may stubbornly refuse to start or else burn spitefully with a sooty yellow flame.

Because of the high volatility of white gas, it is potentially more hazardous than kerosene. Yet because of the greater ease of operation of gasoline stoves, they are the choice of most backpackers.

Butane and Propane

For the ultimate in convenience and ease of operation, the bottled-gas stove is hard to beat. You merely open a valve and light the burner. No priming, no pumping, no flare-up. Butane and propane stoves burn cleanly, and—properly handled—are quite safe. They operate quietly and can be turned way down for simmering.

With all these good points, why aren't bottled gas stoves used by all backpackers? Well, the gas cartridges aren't everywhere available, especially

Accessories for a white gas stove include a fuel bottle, a plastic medicine dropper for priming, a funnel for filling, and matches for lighting. A windscreen helps keep the fire burning hotly, and the stove-container top can double as a cook pot. One compact model of bottled gas stove attaches directly to the fuel container. A "sparker" lighter, wire pricker (for orifice cleaning), and a home-made, lightweight aluminum windscreen complete the ensemble.

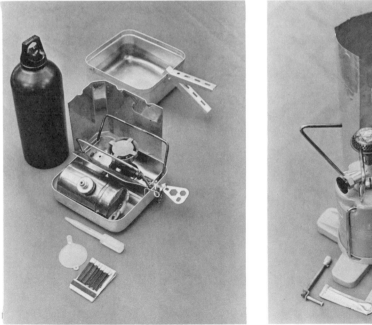

out of the United States, and they are relatively expensive. Though the stoves cost less than gasoline or kerosene types, they also generate less heat, which means you have to operate them longer to prepare a meal. Finally, as the gas pressure in a cartridge decreases with use, the stove's efficiency drops, which means longer burning time.

Alcohol and Solid Fuels

A few stoves—very few—burn alcohol, which puts out much less heat than the other liquid fuels. On the plus side, alcohol burns clean and is not highly volatile, but these features hardly compensate for its low efficiency.

Seldom used by backpackers are stoves that use solid fuels—tablets, pellets, jellies, and such. They provide barely enough warmth to singe a chicken, certainly not enough to boil water.

Using a Stove

You've probably seen an experienced backpacker fire up a precious noodle-encrusted stove. A few deft hand motions, some mumbled incantations, and a cheery flame springs to life. Easiest thing in the world, you say to yourself. But when you try starting your shiny new Super Flame-Thrower you use all your matches, singe your eyebrows, burn a hole in your pants, and end up with a stove as cold as yesterday's oatmeal.

Few things are as exasperating as trying to start a balky backpacking stove. The printed instructions provided with a new stove are of marginal help, since they tell how to get the thing going under optimum conditions: a warm, dry, windless afternoon, at sea level. Of course, the only place you're likely to find such conditions is at home, so home is the best place to fire up a virgin stove. Go by the instructions the first time or two; they'll at least get you off on the right foot. From there on you'll develop your own techniques and your own incantations that will work anywhere in the backcountry. Usually.

Common sense tells you that any stove needs a level base so it won't tip over, shelter from wind to keep it lit, and ventilation to burn properly. A stable, flat rock is ideal for a base. Next best is flat, solid ground, swept clear of leaves and other burnable material. Find wind shelter on the lee side of boulders, or string up a tarp windbreak to shield your kitchen, or arrange a rock "fireplace" around your stove. Most stoves are equipped with windscreens, or baffles, and some of them work. Cooking outdoors, you'll usually have more than enough ventilation. If you must use a stove in a tent, be sure the tent's vents and flaps are open. A stove needs oxygen, and so do you.

A backpacker's stove should be set on a flat rock or bare ground, far from leaves and other burnable material.

"Fill" a gasoline or kerosene stove by pouring fuel carefully into the tank until it's only about three quarters full. A completely topped-off tank may not build up enough pressure. If the filling hole is tiny, as most are, use a funnel to avoid slopping fuel. If you do spill some, clean it up or wait until it evaporates before lighting a match. When the filling operation is completed, replace the fuel container cap and set the container several feet away from the stove.

Most kerosene or liquid gas stoves require priming. This is the process of preheating the burner so that the emerging gas is vaporized prior to igniting. Before priming the stove, be sure to replace its tank cap. On a sleepy morning I once neglected to cap the tank on a gasoline stove, and when the fuel in the priming cup ignited, a bellowing *whoosh* brought me to nerve-shattering wakefulness. Luckily that's all that happened.

To prevent flare-ups, don't overprime. If the burner doesn't light with one priming, make sure all flame is out, then repeat the operation using fuel taken from the container, not from the stove tank. A plastic medicine dropper or small rubber syringe works well for priming.

It's good practice to fuel your stove before each use to assure its operation throughout the preparation of a meal. Also, opening the fuel tank releases any vacuum that may have been induced with cooling. If a stove burns itself dry, don't—repeat, *don't*—refuel it while the burner is hot. Stove as well as fuel bottle may flame up like a torch.

A stove that won't light, or goes out when it has plenty of fuel, or makes coughing noises as it burns may be dirty. Usually, only the orifice is plugged, and it can be cleared with a thin wire made for this purpose. But if things are really clogged, you may have to dismantle and clean the works.

Kerosene stoves are usually primed with alcohol, which lights quickly. They are also equipped with pumps for building pressure inside the tank to force fuel up to the burner. You can buy a small pump to fit a gasoline stove and facilitate the priming operation.

Compared with gasoline or kerosene stoves, cartridge (bottled gas) stoves are a snap to operate. Following the manufacturer's instructions, attach the proper cartridge securely. If the canister feels frosty or you hear a hissing sound, there may be a gas leak, and you should check for a secure attachment between cartridge and stove.

With some bottled gas stoves you can remove a partially empty cartridge. Others cannot be separated from the canister until the contents are completely used up. Be sure you know what can or cannot be done before doing it.

Almost any backpacking stove—be it gasoline, kerosene, or bottled gas—may work sluggishly at low temperatures. Cold inhibits the buildup of internal tank pressure, which is necessary to start fuel flowing to the burner. In really cold weather, keep the fuel tank warm by sleeping with your stove or carrying it close to your body. You'll appreciate the slight inconvenience when you go to fire it up.

A question often asked is, "How much fuel is needed for a trip of such-and-such duration?" It's a reasonable question, but one that has no good answer because so many variables are involved. Experience is the best guide. Start with a full fuel tank or cartridge and, while taking short trips, keep track of how many breakfasts and how many dinners you can cook before having to refuel. That'll give you a rough starting point. But remember that different types of stoves, different *makes* of stoves, require different times to do the same job. Also, cold weather necessitates a longer cooking time than warm weather, as does increasing altitude.

Fuel containers come in a variety of shapes (round, oval, rectangular cross-section), sizes (from .3 liter to 1 liter), and materials (aluminum, tinned steel, plastic). Whatever your choice, **a fuel container must not leak.**

Accessories and Extras

Bottled gas comes in its own one-time-use canister. Gasoline and kerosene must be carried in something that you fill from a larger source. For this you can choose among aluminum bottles, steel cans, or plastic containers. Some containers have built-in pouring spouts; others should be used with a small funnel so fuel isn't spilled. The cap on any container should seal tightly, otherwise your pack will smell like a garage.

Some stoves are equipped with a windscreen; others require a little inventiveness on the owner's part. A few inventions are marvels to behold, such as a cylinder of stiff foil that fits loosely around the stove, or a two-pound coffee can with open ends. But remember, any windscreen must allow ventilation around the fuel tank to avoid overheating.

A plastic medicine dropper is invaluable for priming a stove, and any non-self-cleaning stove should have a wire pricker taped to its bottom, handy at all times.

For winter cooking you should set a stove on a square of Ensolite to keep the cold ground or the snow from chilling the fuel tank.

And don't forget matches—plenty of dry matches stowed in your pack, away from fuel and stove. In addition to matches, I carry a "sparker" lighter, a flint-and-ratchet-wheel affair that ignites the fuel with a flick of the thumb. You can find these in sporting goods stores.

Choosing a Stove

With a few exceptions, most backpacking stoves on the market are "good." Not necessarily good for everything (or everyone), but good in one area of use or another. If a stove's area of use answers most of your needs, then it's the stove for you regardless of what anyone else uses, recommends, or says. Like no other piece of outdooring gear, a stove is a very personal thing, and mature, sober adults have come close to trading blows in defending their own favorites.

Because performance is what counts most in a backpacking stove, people who use stoves a lot are usually more knowledgeable about them than even a savvy salesperson who has never ventured out of the store. Observe different stoves in use. Ask questions of their owners. You may not receive wholly objective answers, but the replies will give you a little something to weigh.

Field-test a few borrowed or rented models. If possible, try them in wind and in cold weather, cooking different kinds of meals. Only after acquiring a feel for actually using a stove should you start shopping around in stores.

To aid your decision-making, jot down some guidelines and rate models according to such criteria as weight, bulk, stability, fuel availability, ease of operation, durability, boiling speed, cold-weather performance, reliability, and cost. Some stoves will rate high in certain areas, low in others; those measuring highest in the areas most important to you are worth a second look. Eventually you'll narrow the field down to one, and that will be the stove for you.

Buying a stove? Look at all models available. Talk with savvy salespersons and experienced backpackers. Evaluate models as to weight, bulk, ease of operation, and cold-weather performance.

COOKWARE AND UTENSILS

To prepare hot foods you usually start by boiling water. To boil water you need a metal vessel. The most basic, as well as compact, vessel is an aluminum or stainless steel cup, which works all right for one person who doesn't consume much at any one time or who doesn't mind heating cup after cup to keep a meal going. For more efficiency you might consider a set of small nesting pots with lids (which keep bugs out and hold heat in). For bigger meals or for more people there are larger pots.

My pressure-cooker friend doesn't mind packing the weight and bulk of her favorite piece of cookware, because food fixed in a pressure cooker is ready in a relatively short time whether you're at sea level or high in the mountains. Less cooking time means a savings in fuel.

"And it makes the rice more digestible," she claims.

I once had a Boy Scout mess kit that consisted of two pots, a cup, and a fry pan, all cleverly nested together. Not once did I ever use the fry pan. It always seemed an unnecessary item, as I've been able to scramble eggs and even sauté fish in a shallow pot without too much difficulty.

A pot without a handle can be picked up with a small pair of pliers or a pot gripper—a lightweight clamp designed especially for this purpose.

Fishing backpackers often tote a lightweight grill for cooking their catch over coals.

As for utensils, except for your pocketknife all you need is a spoon. Forks and table knives are extra baggage, as just about anything you'll be cooking and eating in the backcountry can be managed with a spoon. If meals are to serve several people, you might also want a large spoon for stirring and serving. And if you're a pancake fancier, you might include a small spatula.

When you cook solo, you can eat right from the pot. Otherwise bring along a plastic bowl.

For kitchen cleanup all you need is a pot scrubber—an abrasive, nonmetallic, soapless scouring cloth. No dishwashing soap or detergent, both of which pollute water and soil. Not even the so-called biodegradable soaps are necessary. Hot water, a pot scrubber, and elbow grease (applied away from the water source) will get any pot gleaming clean. But be sure you rinse pots and utensils well with hot, hot water to rid them of diarrhea-causing bacteria. No dishtowel for drying—shake utensils dry, or use a bandanna if you must.

A can opener? In most surplus and outdooring stores you can find a tiny device known as a G.I. opener. So small a gadget is it that some outdoors people wear theirs on a neck chain like an amulet. Despite its size, a G.I. opener works like a charm. If you can't find one, make sure your pocketknife has an opener.

Lightweight and sturdy, a pot gripper holds tightly and prevents burned fingers.

Basic cookware and utensils comprise a single pot with a lid, a cup, and a spoon. But for more versatility in camp cuisine, your kitchen might include nesting pots, a bowl, a cup, knife-fork-and-spoon set, a pot gripper, a G.I. can opener.

Polyethylene water bottles can be carried in an outside pocket of your backpack or clipped to your belt. Most hold a quart of liquid.

Mechanical water filters and purifiers strain out Giardia, protozoa, parasites, bacteria, and fungi, making water safe to drink almost anywhere in the world.

Speaking of pocketknives, a good one should have—in addition to a can opener—a sharp blade or two, a screwdriver, and a pointed tool for making holes. Corkscrews, fingernail files, scissors, saws, and earspoons are optional.

Finally, you'll need something for carrying water. A metal canteen is heavier than a plastic water bottle, and if dented too many times it may spring a leak. With a plastic bottle you can see the level of the liquid inside. Wide-mouth plastic bottles are usually preferable because you can mix dry lemonade and such in them more easily than in the narrow-mouth variety.

One other nonessential but useful object is a one- or two-gallon collapsible water bag. You don't carry it full when you're hiking, unless you like hauling dead weight, but use it in camp to keep from having to run to the water source several times during an evening. There's a boxy model you set on the ground or on a rock, and there's a baggy affair you hang up. Both have spigots that work just like a faucet. Very handy items.

ABOUT MEALS

You needn't change your eating habits when backpacking. If you're a regular sort of person when it comes to dining—that is, if you prefer three squares a day—plan for breakfast, lunch, and dinner each day you're out, plus snacking fare to keep your inner furnace stoked between meals. If at home you're a nibbler throughout the day, continue the same way in the wild, but hold back enough food for a good main meal in the evening.

During an extended backpacking trip, what flesh and blood need more than anything else to keep going is calories, plenty of calories. If your system isn't supplied with 2,500 to 5,000 calories a day it will grow faint. Now, 4,000 calories figures out to be 1½ to 2 pounds of food. So five days of backpacking means toting 7 to 10 pounds of nourishment, ten days means 15 to 20 pounds, and so on. Oh, yes, on any trip of two or more days' duration, it's a good idea to carry a day's worth of extra food, just in case the jaunt lasts a little longer than planned.

Unless you're a Sherpa or a masochist, a two-week food supply, plus clothing and other basic gear, is about all you'll want to carry on your back. Beyond that you should have food cached along the route or else arrange to have it dropped off at predetermined places.

On a week's trek, food can easily account for a fourth of the bulk and a fourth of the weight of your pack. On a longer trip, clothing and other basic gear may not change greatly, but *half* your load may be in edibles. Therefore, in preparing your pack, it behooves you to select foods that have the least weight and bulk for the highest nutritional value.

How to further cut down on weight and bulk? Go easy on canned items, which are very heavy. Discard most of the outer cardboard and paper packaging in which many foods come, saving only cooking directions. Squeeze air out of food bags so they'll take up less space. Avoid fresh fruits and vegetables on treks lasting longer than a day or two; they may be tasty, but their weight adds up fast.

If money is of no concern, you can load your food bag with complete freeze-dried meals, vacuum packed in plastic, foil, and paper. Available in outdooring stores, they are lightweight, reasonably nutritious, and costly. But being near-fanatics about saving a buck wherever they can, most backpackers take great pride in making up menus with food products they pull right off the supermarket shelves. Also, in the woods most backpackers seem to thrive on semi-junk food that at home they wouldn't touch with an eleven-foot pole. Such foods may not be brimming with vitamins and minerals, but most are loaded with carbohydrates, which provide calories by the carload, and so are fine for a few days. Adding a few fat- and protein-rich items will round out the diet nicely.

Breakfasts

Eat breakfast! Eat a hearty, carbohydrate-loaded breakfast! Often the biggest push of the day is in the morning, and for that early effort the body needs plenty of quick nourishment. If the weather is cold, get something rich and hot into your stomach soon after you rise to warm you up and to provide a good shot of energy.

Here are some breakfast suggestions:
- "Instant breakfasts" (add water and drink them down)
- Instant oatmeal (the old outdooring standby, even though it's often likened to wallpaper paste) or other cereals requiring little or no cooking
- Granola (best with nuts and raisins)
- Muesli (a packaged Swiss concoction containing cereals, nuts, and fruit)
- Pancake mix (just add water)
- Eggs (freeze-dried, *not* fresh)
- "Breakfast bars" ("Taste like sawdust," advises one backpacking partner, who nevertheless dotes on them)

Freeze-dried and dehydrated meals may be relatively costly, but they are convenient and, by and large, tasty.

- Beef jerky or beef sticks (cut them up in cereals, or just gnaw on them)
- Dried fruits (delicious chopped and added to cereals)
- Powdered or instant milk (use by itself, or stir into cereals)
- Malted milk powder (mix with instant milk, or sprinkle on cereals)
- Wheat germ (mix with anything)
- Brown sugar (for cereals and drinks)
- Margarine (stir into hot cereals, or use on pancakes)
- Honey or jam (in squeeze tubes—see end of this chapter)
- Instant tea, coffee, cocoa (mix coffee and cocoa to make a tasty café mocha)

Lunches and Snacks

Snacks keep your blood sugar at a constantly high level, which keeps *you* going. You may feel best snacking throughout the day, hardly pausing for a sit-down lunch. But whether lunch is a formal affair or just another in a long series of mouthfuls, keep the food close at hand so you can get at it without having to unload your entire pack. Lunch foods shouldn't require heating, unless something hot is needed to ward off a winter chill.

Some lunch and snack ideas:
- Salted wheat crackers (or pilot crackers, which hold up well in a pack)
- Bread (solid kinds, such as cocktail rye and pumpernickel)
- Margarine (use on bread or crackers)
- Cheese (cheddar, jack, or other firm kinds)
- Salami or summer sausage (whole, unsliced, for best keeping)
- Beef jerky or beef sticks (they keep indefinitely)
- Canned meats (tuna, sardines, kippered herring, corned beef, deviled meats)
- Instant soup or bouillon (if you need a hot drink)
- Nuts (Brazil nuts have high oil content, good for the body's fat needs)
- Peanut butter (homogenized types don't separate from their oils)
- Spun honey (also called whipped honey, it doesn't become runny even when warm)
- Mixed dried fruits (apricots, peaches, pears, apples, bananas, raisins, prunes)
- Fruitcake or nut bread (solid cakes hold together best)
- Cookies (Fig Newtons are especially rich and tasty)
- Hard or chewy candy (keep handy in a pants or jacket pocket)
- Candy bars (or "energy bars," available in natural foods stores)
- Fruit drink mixes (lemonade, orange, punch)

Dinners

Dinner is the main meal of the day. It should be plentiful, rich in protein, and hot. Don't rush through dinner. Enjoy preparing it. Enjoy eating it. Enjoy digesting it.

Some dinner suggestions:
- Instant soups or bouillon (for a first course, to get liquid back into your system)
- Asian noodle soup (it's thick and tasty)
- Packaged noodle meals (add nuts for texture and more protein)
- Packaged rice meals (available in various flavors)
- Dried bean curd (available in Asian markets, to add to soups)
- Dried shrimp (available in Asian markets, to add to soups)
- Beef jerky or beef sticks (cut up in noodle or rice meals)
- Canned fish (tuna, sardines, herring)
- Instant mashed potatoes (add spices for flavor)
- Gravy mixes (use sparingly; some are very salty)
- Cheese (add to noodle and rice meals)
- Dehydrated mushrooms (add to anything)
- Bread (cocktail rye, pumpernickel)
- Margarine (in potatoes, on bread)
- Onion and garlic flakes, other herbs and spices (for flavoring)
- Cookies (chewy kinds hold up best)
- Instant pudding (stir in milk and water; let sit until clotted)
- Instant milk (for puddings, mashed potatoes, soups)
- Tea, coffee, cocoa (for variety, try various herb teas)

Gorp and Glop

After hiking shoes, gorp can be the backpacker's best friend. A mixture of tasty and nourishing items, gorp is a trail snack that keeps mind and mouth occupied when there's nothing else to do but march and munch. The word's origins are as obscure as its ingredients are varied. Some people claim the letters stand for "*g*ood *o*ld *r*aisins and *p*eanuts"; others say the word is the sound made when the stuff is eaten. Whatever, gorp is a backcountry staple, and an addictive one. A friend of mine keeps a small stuff sack of it dangling from his belt at all times, even when he's on big-city streets. "Never can tell when I might need a handful," he says, munching.

Gorp's basic ingredients are nuts, raisins, and chocolate bits mixed in no particular ratio. For variations you can add shredded or toasted coconut,

An ideal backpacker's kitchen: a large flat rock at waist height.

husked seeds (such as sesame, pumpkin, sunflower), chopped dry fruit, granola, or anything else dry and edible that comes to hand.

I once dropped a sack of gorp, spilling half of it on the forest floor. Reluctant to lose so much, I pushed most of it back into the bag, then continued to pick up stray morsels and pop them into my mouth. Detecting a distinct non-gorp taste, I suddenly realized I was standing on a game trail and not all the chocolate bits were what they seemed to be. My appetite for gorp was lost for all of two hours.

Glop is a food of another flavor. Almost always a dinner, because of its heartiness, it's a blending of several things edible that, it is hoped, results in a tasty whole. For example, a basic macaroni-and-cheese dinner can be blended with mushrooms, tuna, and vegetable soup. Or mashed potatoes can be stirred up with onion soup, Vienna sausage, cheese chunks, and nuts. Some glops are more successful than others, so when you hit on a good aggregate, remember the combination.

To make an excellent all-around meal mix at home, combine in a large bowl: ½ cup Grape Nuts; 1 cup rolled oats; ½ cup protein concentrate; ½ cup wheat germ; 1 cup wheat flakes; 4 cups powdered milk; ½ cup brown sugar; 1 cup raisins or chopped apricots; 1 cup chopped pecans; 1 cup 100 percent bran.

Keep the mix in one or more plastic bags. No cooking is required. For any meal, just measure out a cupful, add hot or cold water, and stir well to dissolve the powdered milk. It's good, and it's nutritious.

Packaging and Packing

Packaging meals for just a day hike or a weekend trip need involve nothing more elaborate than brown-bagging—stowing everything in paper sacks or plastic bags and remembering what's been packed for each meal. However, for longer hauls, a tighter organization is advisable so you don't gobble a whole week's lunches the second day out. Rather than dumping all your food into one big stuff sack and rummaging around in it at mealtime to see what you come up with, decide on some organizational scheme at home, and pack accordingly.

One way is to have a heavy-duty plastic bag or stuff sack for each day's edibles. That is, five days, five bags. Or you might have three stuff sacks: one containing only breakfasts; another, lunches; the third, dinners. Whatever scheme you follow, it's a good idea to measure out and package individual meals in plastic bags, which you then put into the main sacks. That way everything will be at hand when you need it, and you won't eat ahead of yourself and have to spend the last days of your trek browsing meadow grass.

Lightweight foods can be stowed in the thin plastic bags you save from trips to your supermarket's produce department. After packaging, squeeze out all the air and close the bag with a rubber band or wire twist. For bulky foods, use freezer bags, which are stronger, or turkey roasting bags, which are surprisingly tough. Squashable foods can go in rigid polyethylene boxes, widemouth bottles, or canisters (available in supermarkets), and squishy things such as peanut butter, margarine, and honey are best carried in plastic squeeze tubes that you fill from the bottom and then seal with a clothespinlike clip. Squeeze tubes (outdooring stores have them) are also handy containers for many dry items: powdered milk, instant coffee, loose tea, granulated sugar, cocoa.

Ground cloth, sleeping pad, and sleeping bag can create a spartan but comfortable campsite almost anywhere. Frost or dew may dampen your gear but needn't quench your spirits.

Bedding
and Slumbering

And now, having meticulously planned your wilderness trek, clothed your body for the occasion, transported gear and self into the outback, found a cozy spot to settle, made a proper camp, lingered over the day's last cup of tea, and yawned hugely into the night for the eighth time, the moment of truth has arrived. You're ready for bed.

Unless you've lugged along a cot or a hammock—which some individuals have been known to do—your bed is going to be Mother Earth. The ground. The same ground you've had underfoot all day. How well you sleep on that ground depends on how well your body can adapt to it. And the factor most important to your adapting is heat loss. When your body loses heat, you get cold. If you're cold, you're uncomfortable. And if you're uncomfortable, you won't sleep.

Usually the temperature of the ground is lower than your body temperature, which means if you lie directly on the earth it's going to conduct heat from you as surely as water drains out of a bathtub when the stopper is pulled. To minimize this kind of heat loss you must insulate your body from the ground.

ABOUT SLEEPING PADS

A sleeping pad is what you lie on, instead of the bare ground, to decrease conduction heat loss. A sleeping pad also makes lumps and bumps more bearable, but most important it insulates you from the chilly earth. But, you cry out, doesn't a sleeping bag insulate? Yes and no. Yes, a sleeping bag insulates where it's fluffed up over you. No, where it's squashed down flat under you. Beneath your body you need something that won't squash down: a sleeping pad.

Three types of sleeping pads are commonly found in outdooring stores: closed-cell types, open-cell types, and air mattresses. Each comes in enough different materials, widths, lengths, densities, and thicknesses to satisfy the most fussy sleeper.

Closed-cell Pads

Closed-cell pads contain thousands of tiny sealed bubbles. Because the cells are sealed, such pads will float on water but not absorb water. In other words, the dead air, or gas, held in the bubbles insulates from ground damp as well as ground chill.

The most popular closed-cell type of pad is known by its trade name, Ensolite. At least three kinds of Ensolite are used for sleeping pads, ranging in color from white to beige to green, and varying in their resistance to cracking in cold weather. Other closed-cell pads are made from polyethylene foams, which are not as flexible as Ensolite, and ethylene-vinyl-acetate foams, which are more durable than Ensolite. All are good insulators, and all come in varying thicknesses.

Open-cell Pads

Open-cell pads contain unsealed bubbles, which makes them spongy and thus more comfortable than closed-cell types. But being spongy, they soak up water like giant blotters. Therefore, open-cell pads are best used in dry-climate areas. To help keep moisture out, open-cell pads usually have a layer or two of waterproof fabric on one or both sides, which adds to their weight and their expense.

A sleeping pad insulates and cushions your body. Pads range from closed-cell varieties, to open-cell types, to combinations of the two, to self-inflating air mattresses containing pads.

Sleeping Pad Sizes

Sleeping pads are generally 20 to 24 inches wide. That doesn't allow much space for thrashing around, but it's enough for resting quietly. If you're used to slumbering in a king- or queen-sized bed, you'll find that a sleeping pad takes a little getting used to. Much rolling and tossing and you may wake up on bare ground, several feet away from your pad. To minimize such nocturnal travels, wedge yourself in place with shoes, pack, or a couple of rocks.

Sleeping pads 72 inches in length give head-to-heel support for anyone other than a junior giant. However, most backpackers prefer a length of 40 to 44 inches, which reaches from about head to knee. If their lower extremities get cold, they put folded clothing under their legs and feet.

Sleeping pad thicknesses vary from ¼ inch to ¾ inch for closed-cell, 1 inch to 2 inches for open-cell. The thinner the pad, the less weight and bulk. The thicker the pad, the more insulation and padding.

Air Mattresses

Not too many years ago air mattresses were the only trail bed available. Though still popular with car campers, who don't care about weight, air mattresses are seldom used by backpackers who count ounces. In addition to weighing more than an equal-sized open- or closed-cell pad, air mattresses are notoriously poor insulators. Instead of the trapped air's warming to body temperature, it cools to ground or air temperature, thus sucking heat from your body. Some air-mattress defenders claim that slipping an Ensolite pad between them and the mattress insulates beautifully, but why lug around both a pad and a mattress? Besides, a repair kit is needed for mending punctures and slow leaks. And inflating one of the things with lung power, especially at high altitudes, can give you a purple face and palpitations.

Overcoming most of these negative features, the Therm-a-Rest foam-filled air mattress provides good comfort and insulation and even self-inflates. No puffing, no huffing—you just unroll it, wait a couple of minutes while it sucks air in, then enjoy.

Offering maximum comfort and excellent thermal insulation, the Therm-a-Rest sleeping pad inflates itself as it's unrolled.

Sleeping Pad Care

Some backpackers seem to take pride in sleeping on a pad that looks like something the cat dragged through the door. Granted that outdooring gear doesn't stay pristine for long, a sleeping pad doesn't have to be grungy to be comfortable. Ground-in dirt, charcoal smears, and food stains will shorten its life and rub off onto a sleeping bag. Soap and water will take care of most soiled spots, but avoid cleaning fluids, which may damage the pad.

Ultraviolet radiation will also shorten the life of a sleeping pad, so whether it's flat or rolled, protect it from direct sunlight.

GROUND CLOTHS

You can unroll your sleeping pad directly on the ground. Plenty of hikers do. But you're better insulated from cold and damp if you first spread out a ground cloth (some call it a ground*sheet*), flatten your pad on it, and then shake your sleeping bag out on the pad.

The cheapest ground cloth is a polyethylene sheet like the drop cloths used by house painters. You can find them in hardware or paint stores. However, being rather fragile, plastic sheets will develop pinholes after a couple of uses, and they are slippery. Better than plastic is coated nylon or a lightweight rubberized fabric. Using your shelter tarp or rain poncho for a ground cloth isn't wise because leaves and stickers may poke holes in the waterproofing.

Ground-cloth size? At least a foot longer and two feet wider than your sleeping pad. Of course, you can go with something bigger. That will give you more ground protection in case you slide off your sleeping pad, or it will permit laying two pads side by side.

A tip: Instead of carrying sleeping pad and ground cloth separately, roll your pad *inside* your ground cloth and secure the combined roll on your backpack. That way you'll have one bundle instead of two, and your pad will be better protected.

ABOUT SLEEPING BAGS

The first thing you should know about sleeping bags is that a halfway decent one is going to cost a pretty penny. It will probably represent the biggest chunk of cash you lay out for camping equipment, so get used to the idea right off.

Ground cloth, sleeping pad, and
bivouac sack can all be rolled up
together into an easily carried bundle.

For most other items—shelter, clothing, cooking gear—you can improvise or compromise, but a sleeping bag is a sleeping bag and nothing else can take its place.

The function of a sleeping bag is to maintain body temperature within a comfortable range during sleep. A sleeping bag minimizes heat loss by providing a layer of insulation between the body and the colder air. Whatever the insulating material (called filler) in a bag is, it's not the material that keeps you warm but the dead air that's trapped within it.

Shape and Size

Virtually every backpacking sleeping bag has a long zipper running down one side, which makes a grand opening that allows you to get in and out without having to worm your way in through the top. It also lets you have the bag partially open when you're too warm. A bag that has the zipper running completely across the bottom can be opened like a book and laid flat to form a comforter, or can be joined to a matching bag to make a double-sized affair. (A tip: Thread a 12-inch length of half-inch cotton tape through the zipper pull and knot it there. The dangling ends are easy to grab in the dark, when you might need to zip up or down.)

Of the many shapes and styles of sleeping bags, the most common are the rectangular, the barrel, and the mummy. A rectangular bag has straight sides and is squared off at top and bottom; a barrel-shaped bag is also square at top and bottom, but it bulges out at the sides. Both rectangular and barrel bags have open tops that can be closed around the shoulders by a drawstring. A mummy bag is shaped more like the human body—wide at the top, narrow at the bottom. Mummy bags have a drawstring that tightens the opening around the face, keeping shoulders and head warm. Being more or less form-fitting, mummy bags have little empty space inside, which makes for warmer sleeping. Nevertheless, some outdoors people feel claustrophobic in them and prefer the roomier rectangular or barrel configuration.

Most sleeping bags are available in two or three lengths. Of course, the shorter the bag, the lighter the weight, but with too short a bag you won't be able to straighten your legs without jamming your feet into the end. Not only is this uncomfortable but it compresses the bag's filler, which will allow your feet to get cold. A little extra room is good if you like to either snuggle down or really stretch out.

Down Fillers

"Loft" is a word that's tossed around freely in discussions of sleeping bags. Loft is simply the total thickness of dead air trapped by a sleeping bag's filler. Since dead air is what keeps you warm, more loft means less heat loss. That's a generality and there are some exceptions, as you'll see later.

By far the most popular sleeping bag filler is down, the fluffy undercoating of waterfowl feathers. Down does a superior job of insulating. (When was the last time you saw a duck shiver?) Lofting well, it is extremely lightweight, compressible, resilient, and breathable, which means that a down bag packs into a small, easily carried bundle but, when shaken out, fluffs up into a very efficient insulator.

If down is so great as a filler, why consider anything else? A couple of reasons. First is cost. In the mid-1970s the price of down went up—so far up that many backpackers couldn't afford a down bag, or refused to pay the inflated prices, and so turned to other fillers.

Down's greatest disadvantage—some say its only disadvantage—is its worthlessness as an insulator when wet. Picture a wet Persian cat: waterlogged, sopping, cold, miserable. That's how a down sleeping bag is when it's been rained on, and that's how you'll be if you try to sleep in it.

A down sleeping bag is superior in cold, reasonably dry weather, or if you can count on keeping it dry. If most of your backpacking is going to be wet going, down may not be best for you.

Synthetic Fillers

To offset the disadvantages of down as a filler, manufacturers of outdooring gear have developed several kinds of synthetic materials, and some of these have been accepted by even the most hard-nosed, mule-minded, tradition-riddled trail veterans. Showing up under various trade names, man-made materials such as polyester fibers, acrylics, nylon, and olefin are the next best thing to down, according to one respected outdooring equipment house. Though not the final answer, synthetic fillers do a good job in certain situations.

Polyester fill is somewhat like wool in that when wet it still insulates. If you should drop your synthetic-fill sleeping bag into a lake, or have a faulty stuff sack that actually funnels in rain (both these accidents happened to one unfortunate chap on a single trip), you just squeeze most of the water out and tuck yourself in at bedtime. You may sleep damp, but you'll sleep reasonably warm.

A polyester bag costs a lot less, on the average, than a down bag. Also, being less compressible, it provides more insulation and padding between you and the ground. Furthermore, synthetic fillers are reputed to be nonallergenic, a comfort to you if you're bothered by natural feather materials. But being less compressible than a down bag, a polyester bag is bulky. So bulky that backpackers usually can't cram it inside their backpack, where it will displace clothing, food, and such, but instead have to lash it on the outside of the pack, where it resembles a rolled-up mattress tied on a Dust Bowl Ford headed for California.

For the equivalent degree of insulation, polyester is heavier than down, a consideration on a trip where every ounce of weight counts. And, finally, it's believed that even good synthetics do not last as long as good down.

Some all-season backpackers make the best of both worlds, having a down bag for dry weather or for long treks where weight savings are important, and a polyester bag for wet times and soggy places. If you can afford two bags, this system is one way to go.

Combination Fillers

A few sleeping bags combine down and polyester fillers, using the former on top for loft and the latter underneath for padding and ground insulation. The manufacturers claim these bags do everything a sleeping bag should do. They may be right.

Construction

You don't have to be an accredited feather merchant to choose, use, and benefit from a sleeping bag, but a little familiarity with the inner workings will give you a better idea of what you're getting into.

A sleeping bag consists of two fabric bags—called shells—one inside the other with insulating filler fitted in between. Shells for quality backpacking bags are usually made of ripstop nylon, Gore-Tex, or a combination of both. Both fabrics are "breathable"; that is, they allow body moisture to escape.

Whether the filler is down or polyester, it isn't just dumped between the shells. If it were, it would settle in one big lump, probably at the bag's foot. To keep the filler distributed evenly, most down bags contain baffles—thin interior fabric walls that prevent the filler from shifting. Polyester fillers are quilted, sandwiched, or contained in tubes, called batts, that are sewn in place. In the highest quality down or polyester bags, baffles or batts are overlapped to

194

SEWN-THROUGH BAFFLES OR BATTS

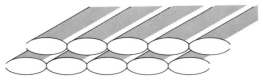

DOUBLE-QUILTED BAFFLES OR BATTS

BOX BAFFLES

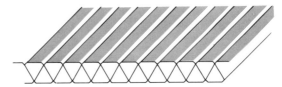

SLANT-BOX BAFFLES

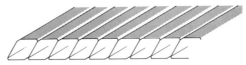

TRIANGLE OR V-TUBE BAFFLES

SANDWICHED BATTS

Sleeping bag baffles or batts are interior compartments that contain down or polyester filler and prevent it from shifting. Overlapping configurations are the most efficient insulators.

eliminate sewn-through seams. Because sewn-through seams create potential cold spots, they are bad news for winter mountaineering.

A zipper baffle, or draft tube, is a long, slim pillow of filler sewn behind the zipper in such a way as to prevent cold from creeping into the closure. It also keeps a sleeper's bare back from coming in contact with the zipper.

A few manufacturers make a sleeping bag containing a vapor barrier liner (or you may be able to buy one to fit your own bag). This is a waterproof inner envelope—a giant plastic bag—that holds body moisture close to your body. A vapor barrier doesn't keep you from sweating, but it does keep the juices from dampening your bag and turning to frost on really cold nights. In a vapor barrier liner you'll sleep considerably warmer than in either a down or a synthetic bag alone.

Accessories

As with most other items of backpacking gear, you can go beyond the basic sleeping bag, adding options and embellishments almost ad infinitum. In so doing, you also add weight and bulk.

A sleeping bag cover is a large sack made to enclose a sleeping bag. Though holding in some warmth, it is designed mainly to help keep the outside of a bag clean. That's all right if you roll far and wide on the ground. But most folks manage to restrict their movements to the surface of their ground cloth and so keep their sleeping bag reasonably clean anyway. Better than a mere cover is a Gore-Tex bivouac sack. It helps keep a bag clean, but, more important, it allows evaporation of body moisture while preventing outside damp from getting in.

Then there are cotton sleeping bag liners. Granted, they feel softer and fluffier on bare skin than a bag's nylon inner shell. But do you need the luxury? And the extra weight? If slumbering in your birthday suit bothers you, slip into lightweight pajamas.

A storage sack is a kind of giant pillowcase designed for storing your sleeping bag loosely at home. That's all right if you can't manage to stow it in some other manner, fluffed up. Another gadget.

Not a gadget is a sleeping-bag stuff sack, a smallish drawstring bag that's best made of coated nylon, into which you cram your down bag or roll your polyester bag for carrying (but *not* for storing). On the trail a sleeping-bag stuff sack makes a compact bundle of your bed, keeping it clean and dry. Stuffed with clothes at night, it makes a handy pillow.

Unless there's something terribly wrong with your neck, a separate pillow is an unnecessary luxury.

Choosing a Sleeping Bag

The humble sleeping bag has a mystic aura about it that somehow causes an otherwise rational adult to lose all sense of practicality and buy far beyond normal human needs. Dazzled by the vast diversity in shapes, sizes, and styles of backcountry bedding, a gentle person living in a temperate climate, whose backpacking treks consist of occasional trail hikes during the summer, will suddenly visualize himself as Robert Peary making a dash for the North Pole and acquire a sleeping bag designed for the land of the midnight sun. A bag in which, turkeylike, he roasts.

Imagining yourself as an intrepid explorer may do great things for your ego, but when it comes right down to selecting a sleeping bag, keep in mind that few people are ever out in 0-degree weather (−18 degrees Celsius). So choose a bag to suit your needs, not your fantasies.

First off, temperature ratings given sleeping bags mean next to nothing. They are very general figures that depend on a great number of variables, not the least of which is the greatest variable of all—one's metabolism. How warm or how cold you sleep depends on your body structure, how you dress (or don't dress) for bed, and what you eat for dinner.

As a general guide, a good mummy bag with 2 pounds of down (4 pounds total weight) will satisfy most spring-to-fall needs across the United States. In the summer such a bag may be a bit warm, in which case you can sleep with it zipped open or else lay it over you, comforter fashion. In late fall a 2-pound bag may need some help, which you can provide by donning socks and long underwear when you tuck yourself in.

If your budget can't bear the cost of down, or if you expect humidity as a constant companion, a synthetic-fill bag might be a better bed for you. A 4½-pound polyester bag will keep most people toasty at 20 to 30 degrees F (−7 to 0 degrees C).

As for shape, a mummy bag is the warmest and also the lightest in weight. A rectangular bag will give you room for tossing and turning, but less warmth, as will a barrel-shaped bag, which is the most spacious (but also the heaviest) of all shapes. Bags without hoods are suitable only for mild-weather backpacking. When the temperature drops, you need plenty of insulation around your shoulders, neck, and head to ward off the shivers.

As a rough indication of quality, check the stitching on a bag, especially along the zipper and around the hood. Tight, straight, even stitching is a fair indication that some care went into the bag's assembly. Another sign of manufacturing care is backstitching at zipper ends, which adds reinforcing where it's needed most.

Press the fabric shells at the foot together between your hands, one inside the bag, the other outside. There should be sufficient loft at the foot so that in use you won't press against the outer shell and create a cold spot.

In the store, fluff a bag by shaking it several times, then get into it, tightening the hood around your face and stretching out your legs. If your feet feel jammed in, try a longer bag. Close and open the zipper, imagining yourself doing it in the dark. The zipper should work from either outside or inside the bag, and it should slide freely without catching in the draft tube. If you're a restless sleeper, see if you can turn over inside the bag, or if you and bag have to turn together (as you must do with a bag whose hood is closed). Either method is okay, but find out which feels better to you.

Sleeping Bag Care

Since a good third of your time outdoors will be splent slumbering, your bed should be kept in a condition that will be conducive to sleep. Besides, if you've paid out a bundle of cash for a sleeping bag, it's only common sense that you make some effort to protect your investment.

Tossing your sleeping bag casually on the bare ground may appear macho, and maybe you really feel you don't need anything else under you, but such nonchalance can lead to a bag's early demise. If you shun a sleeping pad, at least use a ground cloth. It'll protect your bag from abrasion and protect you from dampness during the night. And speaking of dampness, in the morning take time to turn your bag wrong side out and let it air for a while before packing it. Of course, if your bag gets wet, encourage it to dry by shaking it in the open air. After every trip air-dry and fluff up your bag before storing it away.

A little warming sunshine on a sleeping bag does no harm, but leaving a bag in direct sun for very long may lead to damage from excess heat and ultraviolet rays, which can burn the natural oils in down and damage the crimp in synthetic fibers. Beware of open fire. Sparks can melt holes in a bag's outer shell, and flame can ignite the whole works.

Stuff or roll a sleeping bag starting at the foot in order to push air out of the top of the bag. When you remove a bag from a stuff sack, be gentle so you don't damage the baffles. At home avoid hanging a bag, which puts a strain on its baffles. Instead, store it loosely in a large fabric bag or lay it flat so it will "remember" its loft. Don't leave a bag rolled or stuffed for storage. It may not loft when you want it to.

A sleeping bag is a costly investment, so when shopping for one, know your needs and choose carefully. Don't be shy about crawling into a bag in the store; you're the one who is going to be sleeping in it outdoors. Each morning after sleeping in a bag, turn it inside out to dry and air for half an hour.

Cleaning a Sleeping Bag

One bright day you scrutinize your sleeping bag and realize that it no longer has that fresh-from-the-store appearance. The muddy footprints of that overzealous Labrador, the amorphous blobs remaining from that oatmeal breakfast in the sack, the gourd-shaped stain impressed by the back of your head all combine to make your trail bed resemble a sack of overdue laundry. You realize the time has come to clean it.

There are two methods by which a sleeping bag can be purified: dry cleaning or wet washing. Depending on the cleansing agent and the care taken, either method can work like a charm or else be disastrous. *Improper cleaning can ruin a sleeping bag.* As a general rule, a down bag can be either dry cleaned or wet washed; however, a synthetic bag should only be washed because dry cleaning solvents can damage the fibers of a polyester fill. Of course, every rule has an exception. A sleeping bag with a part-cotton shell is best dry cleaned to avoid excessive fabric shrinkage.

If dry cleaning is your choice, don't attempt the job yourself but seek out a firm that knows how to handle a down bag. Where? Ask other backpackers who have had their bags cleaned satisfactorily. Ask around the outdooring stores. But make sure of the firm's competence at cleaning down products before entrusting your bag to them. Improper solvents can destroy the insulating properties of down.

Important note: After a bag has been dry cleaned, air it outside for two or three days to get rid of any traces of cleaning solvent. If you still smell chemicals, continue to air the bag until the smell is completely gone. The fumes of some solvents may be toxic.

Because dry cleaning a bag can be likened to playing Russian roulette, depending on the experience of the person doing it, many backpackers opt to wash their sleeping bags. You might just find a laundry capable of doing a good job; otherwise you can—exercising great care—do it yourself. But remember that a sleeping bag contains, in addition to the filler, delicate fabric baffles that can be damaged by careless handling.

You should wash a sleeping bag in a front-loading, tumble-action machine,

Stuff a down bag into its sack gently, beginning at the foot; roll a polyester bag tightly from bottom to top.

as agitator-type washers are too rough. Using cool or lukewarm water, and no more than three heaping tablespoons of mild soap (not detergent, which is too harsh), run the machine through a complete "delicate fabric" wash cycle, adding more soap if needed for sudsing. After the spin-dry action has stopped, transfer the bag to a commercial-sized drier by gently gathering it into one large bundle. Tender, loving care is especially important at this stage, because when the filler is wet and heavy, rough handling can rip loose the bag's baffles.

Tumble-dry the bag by alternating heat settings between "Low" and "Air" every 15 to 20 minutes until dry. Tumbling with a laceless tennis shoe will help keep the filler from clumping. Finally, air the bag for a couple of days, fluffing and shaking it periodically.

You can also hand-wash your sleeping bag in a few inches of lukewarm water in the bathtub. Pat the suds gently through the bag to wash, and knead it gently in fresh water until the rinse runs clear. Press out excess water, then let the bag drain in the tub for several minutes before moving it to a commercial drier.

SLEEPING TIPS

At one time a sleeping bag was a sleeping bag and you used it to keep yourself warm while sleeping. Today most bags are classified as one-, two-, three-, or four-season bags, meaning their design and insulating properties are such as to make them usable for one or more seasons of the year. But sometimes a winter-weight bag may be too much for summer, and a summer-weight bag may not be enough on a brisk autumn night.

Some backpackers own two bags: a lightweight model for spring and summer use and a medium-weight job for cooler weather. Then when the mercury really drops they slip one bag inside the other and are ready for winter's icy fingers.

Another possibility is a half-bag, also known as an elephant-foot bag, which insulates everything from toes to waist. To keep everything from waist up warm, you don an insulated, hooded parka and, if necessary, mittens. It's a good sleep-out arrangement for an unplanned bivouac, but it's also a favorite with backpackers who are fanatics about saving weight. The half-bag is also an ideal size for youngsters.

When your hiking partner is companionable and willing, zipping two bags together can make for a warm and cozy sleeping arrangement. But not all bags will join up in this fashion. Usually they have to be the same make, one with a lefthand zip, the other with a righthand zip.

You probably won't want to sleep in trail-raunchy clothing inside your bag unless you're desperate for more insulation. On cold-weather trips a better idea is to keep a set of long underwear in the bottom of your sleeping-bag stuff sack where it'll be close at hand if you need it.

If you do bed down clothed, empty your pockets and take off your belt or suspenders. Lying on a pocketknife or belt buckle all night is not very comfortable.

On a really cold night you can prevent some morning frustrations by sharing your sleeping bag with a few inanimate objects such as your contact lenses in their case, your camera, your cookstove, and a water bottle. They won't keep you warm, but your body heat will keep them from freezing.

So much for cold-weather sleeping. If you become too warm in your sleeping bag, unzip it. Flap it open. Stick a leg out. Or get out of the bag altogether and use it on top of you like a blanket.

As beautiful as it may appear, the wilderness can be a hazardous place for a poorly prepared or naïve individual.

Thriving and Surviving

There's never been a shortage of backcountry scare stories. If you pay much attention to the newspapers, it seems that outdooring people are always falling off mountains, perishing in the desert, or being mauled by bears. Such harrowing episodes make sensational reading and help convince stay-at-homes that the wilderness is a terrifying place frequented only by raging animals and deranged humans.

Such mishaps do occur, but they are the exception rather than the rule. Because the majority of wilderness forays are carried off without incident, they don't make tabloid type reading. Except by word of mouth, you seldom hear about good experiences.

Of course, one backpacker may flourish for weeks outdoors, while another may dislocate both ankles donning hiking boots. Does this mean some people are born backpackers while others are natural klutzes? What is it that enables one person to thrive in the wild, another to barely survive?

Outdooring savvy gained by experience is part of the answer. The rest has to do with common sense, which means being prepared mentally and physically for almost any eventuality, being capable of making rational decisions, and being constantly aware.

Each year people die in emergencies that could have been avoided or because they reacted wrongly by not being aware of the nature of the hazard. Many potential hazards in the wild are objective. That is, they simply exist and are by and large meaningless to humans. For example, a snow avalanche may scour a wilderness mountainside clean, but it doesn't constitute any real "danger" to anyone if no one is around. Then there are the subjective hazards, those brought about by the presence or the influence of a human being. Polluted water is no danger to you until you drink it, in which case you may be courting an emergency situation.

It's the subjective situations that should concern you, as a backpacker, because they are the things you can do something about. To forestall most outdooring emergencies you should:

1. Keep in good condition, physically and mentally.
2. Plan ahead.
3. Let someone know of your plans.
4. Carry your essentials kit at all times.

MENTAL ATTITUDES

Some outdoor emergencies are recognized immediately, such as the sudden realization you're disoriented or completely lost. Other situations develop insidiously without recognition, until it's too late to do anything about them. These are the hazards that pose hidden dangers to your life.

Certain mental attitudes carried into the outdoors without your realization may override common sense. Worse yet, they may affect your mental attitude and so interfere with your entire will to live. Let's look at three of these attitudes: overdetermination, get-home-itis, and fear of the unknown.

Overdetermination

Overdetermination is the state of mind that allows long-sought desires to overrule good judgment. It can push a person to use every ounce of energy to attain a goal, leaving none to sustain life once the goal is reached. Overdetermination is characteristic of the gung-ho outdoors person, the individual who is going to get to the top of the mountain, or cover 20 miles in one day, come hell or high water. An overly determined person is often out to prove something. An overly determined person often is highly competitive, wanting to be the first or the fastest.

One false step in the wild can result in an emergency. At all times know what you're doing, and know how to handle a crisis.

Never will all members of a group of backpackers be perfectly matched in their goals, abilities, and interests. Invariably, in any group, one or two people will quickly emerge as overly determined "pushers." They're the ones who'll be first up at the crack of dawn, first to gobble down their breakfast, first to be off and hiking (usually at an antelope's gait), first over obstacles (without waiting to help anyone), and usually first to be heartily hated by everyone else.

In itself, determination provides drive and initiative. Sometimes it can be a saving characteristic (as when it provides the will to survive), but when determination is all-consuming, causing you to become reckless and indifferent to the needs of others, it is a hazard, an impediment to survival.

Get-home-itis

This is a nagging pressure caused by home-related obligations, promises, or responsibilities a person feels must be honored at all costs. In an attempt to respect them, good judgment is often forsaken in the hope that luck will take care of everything else.

But luck is a rare commodity. Depending on it in the wild is playing a dangerous game.

If you're unable to leave your daily worries behind when you head into the backcountry, they may plague your every step. Not only will they spoil your pleasure but, worse yet, they may blur commonsense decisions.

Common Fears

No matter which way a cat is dropped, it supposedly will land on its feet. But when backpacking humans must adjust quickly from a civilized environment, with all its comforts, to an existence much like that of a cave dweller, they often develop psychological problems or fears.

Once while trekking in the Trinity Alps of northern California I managed to put up a shelter just before bad weather closed in. Dry and comfortable in my sleeping bag, I watched the storm rage. Idly—and for no reason other than want of something more constructive to do—I began thinking of some of the terrible things that could befall me. I could be struck by lightning (it was flashing all around). I could be crushed by a toppling tree (they were swaying wildly in the wind). I could be attacked by a bear (though there probably were no bears within 500 miles). I could be carried away by a landslide (rain was falling in torrents). I could be seized by Bigfoot (a local cousin of the Abominable Snowman).

With such cheerful thoughts in mind, I worried for all of ten seconds. Then, after laughing aloud at such fears of the unknown, I rolled over and promptly fell asleep.

Realizing that you most likely will have fears, and that fears are normal emotions in unfamiliar situations, you'll be aware of them. And you'll be better able to cope with them as they appear. Fears can be expected in any outdoor situation. In addition to fear of the unknown, and fear of your ability to cope with the situation, you may experience other fears:

Aloneness
If you're at all a sociable human, the thought of being without companions, voices, or immediate help may bother you. But being alone has its advantages, as it can be the best way of getting to know yourself.

Darkness
When you can't see, your mind likes to play games. You imagine that out beyond the feeble beam of your flashlight lurk all manner of vile beings ready to have at you the instant your back is turned. But scientists are still attempting to prove the existence of Bigfoot, and there just aren't any monsters.

Wild Animals
Some folks assume that all feathered and furry critters are out to get them. But except for some bears in a few parts of the country, and some snakes in a few other parts, there really aren't any animals harmful to humans. When in the territory of bears or snakes, follow the commonsense precautions given earlier, which involve letting them know of your presence so they can make a dignified retreat. Generally, animals are more anxious to avoid you than you are them. Contrary to popular belief, snakes do not crawl into sleeping bags or tents.

Society
You've bid family and friends good-bye and are off for a week in the wild. On your second day out a freak storm dumps three feet of snow, and the temperature drops below freezing. In the face of more of the same kind of weather, should you call off the trip? Or are you afraid everyone back home will think you're a softy?

If you are more concerned with what others think than with what feels right to you, you may have a deep, but very real, fear of losing face, of admitting failure. When wrestling with such emotions, just remember that *you* know what the situation is; no one at home does. You are the one whose well-being is at stake, so in the interest of self-preservation act accordingly.

Such basic fears cause stress, and under stress humans aren't always at their best. Fear and imagination plague almost every person who is face-to-face with crisis, but fearfulness that can turn to blind panic may cause even experienced, knowledgeable persons to injure or kill themselves in the intensity of terror. Fear may well be responsible for more deaths than exposure or hunger.

Fear and stress also cause physiological reactions. Adrenaline is released; muscles tense; abdominal blood vessels contract to drive extra blood to the muscles. The liver releases stores of glucose as fuel. Although these reactions prepare the body for handling the stress-causing situation, they use great quantities of the body's limited supply of available energy and are therefore physically exhausting.

A few individuals claim they never feel fear and chuckle at others who do. But fear can be a healthy reaction, because it reminds you to be cautious rather than reckless. Don't be afraid of fear. Accept it for what it is, and respond to it constructively.

PHYSIOLOGICAL CONSIDERATIONS

Backpacking is traveling under your own muscle power, which produces heat by burning available energy. This energy is derived from food and water and is converted to glycogen, some of which the body stores as reserve. Some is also converted to sugar, which is held in the muscles for quick use.

You travel primarily on those sugars held in your muscles. As these sugars are used up, heat, lactic acid, and carbon dioxide are produced. The latter two are detrimental by-products, and they are flushed out of your system. But if strenuous muscle activity produces these by-products faster than they can be dissipated, your body can become oversaturated, resulting in muscle failure or fatigue.

Dealing with Fatigue

The feeling of muscle fatigue may cause great concern the first time you're aware of it. You may be limp as a wet noodle, totally wrung out. Your legs and arms may refuse to function, no matter how much you will them to. Such

When you feel tired, stop and rest to allow your body to rid itself of lactic acid buildup. To prevent fatigue, get plenty of sleep and eat well.

fatigue will remain until you give your body time to automatically rid itself of the lactic acid buildup and disperse the carbon dioxide.

The most obvious and immediate answer, of course, is rest. When you rest you can rid your system of about a third of the lactic acid buildup in the first five to seven minutes. In another five minutes you get rid of only about 5 percent more, so during the day take short rest stops rather than flaking out altogether, which will cause muscle stiffening. Sometimes fatigued muscles will knot up and cramp painfully. Again, a brief rest is the best cure, though taking salt (either regular table salt or salt tablets) or "athlete's drink" has been known to help.

To help *prevent* fatigue, get a good night's sleep before an active day, and

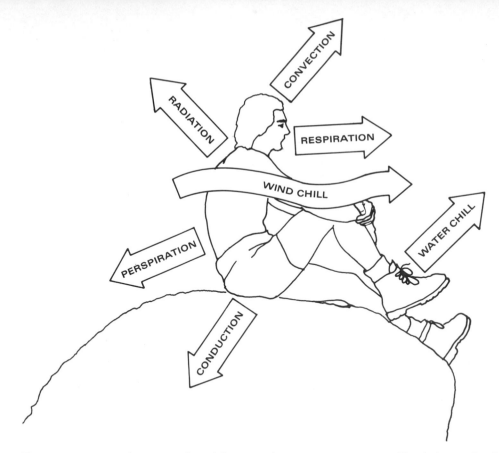

Even on a sunny day a careless hiker can lose great amounts of body heat. Avoid such losses—which can lead to hypothermia—by keeping your body covered, wearing adequate clothing, avoiding prolonged contact with anything cooler than body temperature, and staying dry.

the next morning eat an easily digested, high-carbohydrate breakfast. Start out slowly. Then gradually increase the pace, settling on one you can easily maintain for hours.

Avoiding Heat Loss

As long as your mass of living tissue remains quiet in a still-air, room-temperature environment, it requires little special shelter or energy to maintain a nearly constant temperature of 98.6 degrees F (37 degrees C). But when muscle energy is used, body heat is produced. Too much heat production triggers a message to the control system to open the sweat glands and cool things down through water evaporation. Conversely, if your body becomes too cool, the cold sensors call for the muscles to move (shiver) and produce body heat.

When body temperature falls to around 96 degrees F (36 degrees C), shivering becomes intense and the brain numbs; at about 91 degrees F (33 degrees C), shivering becomes violent; below 86 degrees F (30 degrees C), unconsciousness results. Though your body can lose heat in several ways, as described below, you can prevent this from happening by having the proper outdooring gear and knowing when and how to use it.

Radiation

Radiation is the leading cause of body heat loss. In the open, your natural surface warmth tends to transfer to other surfaces. Minimize such loss by keeping your body covered. Unlikely though it may seem, an unprotected head can cause loss of a third of your total heat production. If you feel chilly, put on a hat.

Conduction

Prolonged contact with fixed solid matter cooler than skin temperature causes body heat loss. Don't sit or lie on the ground or lean against cold rocks unless you insulate yourself with clothing or a sleeping pad.

Convection

Heat is transferred away from your body by air moving over it. The primary function of clothing is to retain a layer of warm air close to the body. Clothing that is too thin or too porous will allow heat to be drawn away from the body, causing what is commonly called wind chill. Wear layers of adequate clothing.

Perspiration

Sweating causes body cooling through evaporation of moisture from the skin. Sweating is caused by too high a temperature and by exertion. Keep your body warm but not hot. Slow down; take things easy.

Respiration

Inhaling cold air and exhaling warm air steals significant body heat. Preheat really cold air before it goes to your lungs by breathing through a scarf or bandanna.

Water Chill

Wet clothing can wick heat away from your body hundreds of times faster than dry clothing. Stay dry. Don't get wet. And wear wool, which is warm even when wet.

The outdoors person always
stays warm.

TREATING COMMON MALADIES

An ounce of prevention is worth several pounds of cure, especially when weighed against a backpacker's potential ailments. As we've been saying all along, being conscientious about doing the right things at the right time will go far in assuring you of good health. Nevertheless, on the off chance that something untoward should happen, you should be able to recognize symptoms —in yourself as well as in others—of the most common outdooring maladies and know how to treat them. Without being unduly gloomy, that's what the following pages of this chapter are about. Anyone going into the wilderness should have a basic knowledge of first aid, as taught by the American National Red Cross; see their latest edition of *Standard First Aid and Personal Safety* (Garden City: Doubleday & Company). For more detailed coverage of back-country doctoring, see the latest edition of *Medicine for Mountaineering,* James A. Wilkerson, editor (Seattle: The Mountaineers).

Altitude Sickness

If you live at or near sea level and set off on a backpacking trek in the mountains, beware of the effects of high altitude. You may feel a bit spacey, kind of headachy. You may tire easily.

Almost everyone is affected to some degree by high altitude. The two main differences in an environment higher than sea level are decreased oxygen content and decreased humidity, as much as 50 percent less oxygen and moisture than that surrounding you at home. When experienced suddenly, these changes can produce nausea, insomnia, diarrhea, shortness of breath, headache, gassiness, and fatigue. Lack of oxygen also impairs judgment. You may think you're doing something right when you're really not. Another symptom of oxygen lack is a reluctance to slow down, to take things easy.

Altitude sickness usually goes away by itself in a few days, as your body becomes used to decreased oxygen. Exertion makes matters worse, so loaf along at first. Work up to altitude gradually. For example, if you expect to spend most of your trip at 10,000 feet, don't go for it all at once. Camp overnight at 5,000 or 6,000 feet before heading higher. Eat lightly, avoiding meals heavy in fats.

A more serious disease of high altitude is pulmonary edema, in which the lungs fill with liquid. Most common in people under age twenty, pulmonary edema can occur any time a person goes higher than 9,000 feet. Its early symptoms are not pleasant: coughing and wheezing, chest pain, spitting of blood, and bubbling sounds in the chest. Because pulmonary edema is often followed by pneumonia, immediate evacuation of the patient to lower altitudes is imperative. If coughing persists, see a physician.

Frostbite

Frostbite, the actual freezing of body tissues, is most common in areas of the body exposed to wind and cold—fingers, toes, nose. Mild frostbite, or frost nip, is characterized by numbness and a whitish, dead-looking coloration; severe frostbite by whiteness and a hard feeling to the affected part.

Do not follow the old housewife's cure by rubbing frostbite with snow or massaging it vigorously to restore circulation. This will damage tissue. Nor should you raise the temperature of the affected area above body temperature. Treat mild frostbite by placing the extremity in contact with a companion's warm crotch, abdomen, or armpit. Treat severe frostbite by rapid rewarming in water heated just enough so that it doesn't burn a hand held in it. The rewarming should be continued until the area regains a healthy color, after which it should be treated as a burn.

Once rewarming has started, the area will be extremely painful, so be prepared with some kind of relief medication. If there is persistent pain, numbness, or discoloration, see a physician as soon as possible to avoid the risk of gangrene.

Thermal Hazards

Both heat exhaustion and heatstroke (also called sunstroke) are caused by exertion at high temperatures. The former is a mild reaction to overheating, salt deficiency, and dehydration that is easily treated by administering liquids; the latter is a serious condition that requires fast, drastic treatment.

In hot weather be aware of your companions' physical conditions as well as your own feelings. The symptoms of heat exhaustion are red face, clammy skin, lightheadedness, irritability, sweating, and palpitations, which can be relieved by taking a rest in a shady spot and drinking plenty of water or juice. Taking table salt, salt tablets, or an "athlete's drink" is essential to restoring the system's balance.

Heatstroke, caused by the production of more body heat than can be dissipated, is characterized by heavy, bounding pulse, hot, dry skin, confusion, and—unless treatment is forthcoming—coma. Body temperature must be lowered immediately by immersing the patient in water or snow, or dousing with water. Recovery should be followed by rest.

Guard against heat exhaustion and heatstroke by taking things easy in hot weather. Take a lesson from the wild animals by "going to ground," resting in the shade, during the hottest time of day. Drink plenty of water, and ingest salt.

Hypothermia

Hypothermia may be a new word to you, but it's the only word that describes the rapid, progressive mental and physical collapse accompanying chilling of the body's inner core. The most common cause of outdooring deaths, hypothermia results from exposure to cold wind, usually coupled with damp, inadequate clothing. So much heat is lost from the body that it cannot be replaced by shivering and muscular activity.

The moment your body begins to lose heat faster than it produces heat, you are undergoing exposure. Two things happen: You voluntarily exercise to stay warm, and your body makes involuntary adjustments to preserve normal temperatures in the vital organs. Both responses drain your energy reserve. The only way to stop the drain is to reduce the degree of exposure.

If exposure continues until your energy reserves are exhausted, cold reaches the brain, depriving you of judgment and reasoning power. *You do not realize this is happening.* Additionally, you lose control of your hands, which makes self-treatment extremely difficult. From there on, things go from bad to

worse. Unless exposure is halted immediately and body heat restored, death
may result within an hour.

To understand hypothermia you should understand cold. Most hypothermia cases develop in air temperatures between 30 and 50 degrees F (0 to 10 degrees C). That may not seem terribly chilly, but wet clothing at 50 degrees F is unbearably cold, and it drains body heat rapidly, especially if any wind is blowing. Avoid exposure and heat loss, as we mentioned earlier in this chapter, by staying dry. Don rain gear before you get wet. Wear wool.

Always be alert for the symptoms of hypothermia:

1. Uncontrollable fits of shivering.
2. Vague, slow, slurred speech.
3. Lapses of memory and incoherence.
4. Fumbling or immobile hands.
5. Stumbling, lurching gait.
6. Drowsiness.
7. Apparent exhaustion.

A person hit with hypothermia may deny it, claiming everything is fine. Believe the evidence, not the person. Even mild symptoms demand immediate drastic treatment:

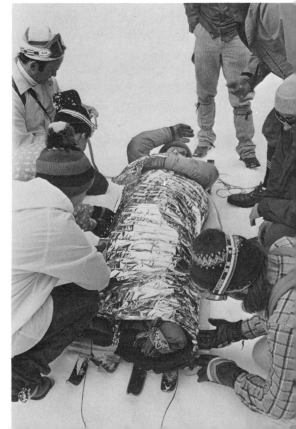

An immobilized person becomes chilled very fast, so bundle an accident victim in plenty of dry clothing. Use a "space blanket" to help retain body heat and protect against dampness.

1. Get the victim out of the wind and wet.
2. Strip off all wet clothing.
3. Get the victim into dry clothes and a warm sleeping bag. If the victim is only mildly impaired, give warm drinks.
4. If the victim is only semiconscious or worse, try to keep him or her awake. Give warm drinks. Put the victim, stripped, into a sleeping bag with another person, also stripped, and maintain body-to-body contact.
5. Build a fire to warm the camp.

You may slip into hypothermia in a matter of minutes. If under existing weather conditions you can't stay warm and dry, you should terminate exposure. Get out of wind and rain. Build a fire. Make camp while you still have a reserve of energy. Eat starches and sugars. Watch carefully for warning symptoms. Never ignore violent shivering. Remember that hypothermia is the number-one outdooring killer.

Stings and Bites

Insect stings and bites are usually nothing more than an annoyance you learn to live with outdoors. Their discomfort can be relieved by applying cold to the painful area for two or three minutes (a cool mud pack often works wonders); taking aspirin may also help. Backpackers with known allergic reactions to stings from bees, wasps, hornets, and yellow jackets should always carry fresh medication in their first-aid kits.

Ticks are flat, leathery, bloodsucking insects that can carry Rocky Mountain Spotted Fever or Lyme's Disease. Remove an embedded tick by grasping its body with tweezers, or stout fingernails, and twisting it as you pull up and out. The spot will probably itch fiercely for days afterward, but try not to scratch it or it might become infected.

Scorpion stings may be quite painful, but are usually not lethal for persons in good health. A victim of scorpion sting should be kept quiet, and the affected part held below heart level. Apply cold locally, and give aspirin to alleviate pain. Obtain medical care as soon as possible.

Despite their reputation, snakes are neither as sinister nor as death-dealing as most people believe. A poisonous snakebite—identified by one or more puncture wounds—is usually followed by localized pain, swelling, and skin discoloration. The victim may feel dizzy and weak. If no such reactions follow a bite, no treatment is needed. Treatment consists of incision and suction to remove venom, plus medical care as soon as possible, as detailed in instructions provided with snakebite kits.

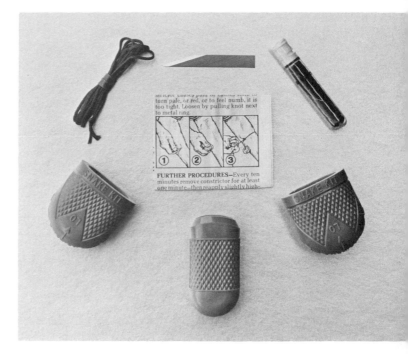

The basic snakebite kit contains disinfectant, a sharp blade for making incisions, a set of suction cups, and a tourniquet. Read the printed instructions carefully and understand them completely before any need arises.

General Illnesses and Injuries

Most illnesses and injuries, such as digestive disorders, colds, strains, sprains, bruises, abrasions, and small cuts, can be treated with items from the first-aid kit. Sufferers of these minor maladies will benefit from a day or two of rest.

A person immobilized by serious injury should not be moved unless threatened by further danger from falling rock or severe weather. Improperly shifting an accident victim may cause additional injury, so, instead, summon help (from a Park Ranger station or County Sheriff's office) for possible evacuation. While some backpackers go for assistance, at least one person should remain with the injured party to administer first aid.

LIVING OFF THE LAND

The best shelter for the backpacker is a tent or tarp. If you're caught out at night or by bad weather, and you have neither, you'll have to improvise with what nature may have to offer. First look for natural shelters that require minimum effort on your part to make them habitable. Caves are ideal; all you need do is move in. You may find a fallen tree whose branches form a sort of covering, or you might crawl into thickets of brush. Protecting the environment is fine at any other time, but in an emergency don't hesitate to cut boughs or break branches for making a lean-to that will baffle or break the wind.

The idea of digging a snow cave or constructing an igloo makes a nice mental picture—you imagine yourself safe and snug within, while storms rage outside—but unless you have waterproof clothing, plus extra dry clothing, plus plenty of food, plus a shovel, forget about making a snow cave. It's cold, wet work that burns up a lot of energy. Instead, look for rocks or branches where snow has drifted but left a hollow that might accommodate you. Often, in deep

A snow cave retains a surprising amount of heat, but digging one is wet work. When seeking emergency shelter, look for natural hollows around rocks or low tree branches.

snow a "well" will be found around the base of a tree that can offer good wind protection.

Except for aborigines, few people are adept enough or know the land well enough to live off it entirely. Sure, there are edible plants and animals in the wild, but you should know all about them *before* the need arises. An emergency situation isn't the time to start experimenting.

You can learn from nature guide books about edible plants and browse your way through such healthy greens as wild mustard, cow parsnip, miner's lettuce, thistle, and cattail, avoiding the likes of hemlock, nightshade, and poison ivy. You can practice snaring rabbits, birds, and snakes. But unless you are competent in living off the land—*really* competent—don't count on it as a sole means of survival. Usually the energy expended in gathering and preparing such natural foods far outweighs the energy gained in eating them. Better to make sure you have extra raisins with you, and supplement them with purslane, rose hips, and—if you must—grasshoppers.

With ample water, you could sit perfectly still and perhaps live for as long as four weeks without food. Not the most appealing way of waiting for rescue, but some people have done it and survived.

Morning light on aspen, one of the visual delights of the backpacking experience.

A Final Few Words

As my friend of few words declared so positively on that mountaintop, there's nothing complicated about backpacking. It's easy. It's fun. It's even addictive. I hope that in the foregoing pages I've guided you out of your living room and headed you toward a mountaintop of your own. But my ideas are only a beginning. Savoring a trek to the next summit or the next valley is all up to you.

As you become more mindful about the techniques and tools of backpacking, pore over the equipment reviews that appear from time to time on the shelves of bookstores and in outdooring shops. I've already mentioned a few specialized publications. Here are several more books of a fundamental nature that are entertaining reading as well as excellent sources of practical information. Look for their latest editions.

Backpacking One Step at a Time by Harvey Manning (New York: Vintage Books).

The Complete Walker by Colin Fletcher (New York: Alfred A. Knopf).

Walking Softly in the Wilderness—The Sierra Club Guide to Backpacking by John Hart (San Francisco: Sierra Club Books).

Wilderness U.S.A. by the National Geographic Society (Washington, D.C.).

As you become more enticed by exotic travel

destinations and untried backpacking lands, look to popular magazines such as *Backpacker, Outside,* and others. Their photographs alone will energize the most listless spirits.

Get on a mailing list for catalogs from L. L. Bean, Recreational Equipment, Inc., and other outdooring suppliers and organized trip planners. Through the pages of such publications you can adventure vicariously before doing it in fact.